THE COMMUNITY THEATRE

The Community Theatre

AND HOW IT WORKS

BY

JOHN WRAY YOUNG

HARPER & BROTHERS, PUBLISHERS, NEW YORK

THE COMMUNITY THEATRE

Library of Congress catalog card number: 57-10361

For MARGARET

whose artistry in design has given added joy
to nearly two hundred productions.

CONTENTS

Prologue

Last June I found a special pleasure in a sunset as the plane leveled off at nine thousand feet and headed for the Southland and home. The speaking tour was over; six appearances and three thousand miles had been quickly accomplished. And yet I knew, as the Ozarks below caught the gold and pink of the fading light, that what I had to say could not wait for the swift facilities of the Air Age.

At each theatre I visited there were too many questions and no time for complete answers. The community groups needed help and guidance; not in the fundamentals of play production, for these were common knowledge in 1956, but in the complex principles of procedure. I had been speaking to established organizations: playhouses which had learned lessons common to all, through the wasteful method of trial and error. But what of the smaller groups, the beginning theatres? Were they to follow this devious, dangerous way of self-teaching?

Before the Convair settled into the landing pattern at the Shreveport Airport, I knew I had to write this book.

For more than twenty-six years my wife, Margaret Mary Young, and I have worked in and for this astounding development of a national expression: the American community theatre. We have seen it struggle and prosper through almost three decades of its brief life. We have come to know what it means to individuals, towns, cities, states, and regions. We begin to see what it *can* mean to America.

Because it is chiefly a volunteer theatre needing trained professional leadership, its immediate want is broad dissemination of not only the *how* of community theatre, but also the *why*. The countless casualties among community groups are almost equally divided between those who never learned *how* to do this special kind of theatre properly and those who failed because they had no understanding of the philosophy upon which the idea is based.

Community theatre is far more than "putting on plays." Let any who consider that the real objective read no further, unless they are willing to consider and learn the precepts of each chapter—both the *why* and the *how*.

I have purposely intertwined the philosophical and the practical because I believe that an understanding of the *one* is essential to consummation of the *other*. I have done this against the exciting and growing backdrop of the growth of the idea from its minuscule beginning in 1912 to the thousands of groups which now cover the land.

The established playhouses will, I trust, learn why they have enjoyed success. The beginning groups may here find a marked path which can lead to permanence. The student who is considering a life in theatre may, and I hope this devoutly, be inspired and informed to try the fine and rugged career of community theatre. And for all those who regard the arts in more detached fashion, I hope that herein they may gain a new understanding and appreciation of this theatre form which may well become one of America's significant contributions to the culture of the world.

J. W. Y.

January 1957

THE COMMUNITY THEATRE

CHAPTER ONE

What Is Community Theatre?

In Jacksonville it's the Little Theatre: in Long Beach it is called the Community Playhouse; Kalamazoo names it The Civic Players; Cedar Rapids has its Footlighters; and Columbus has the Players Club. In other cities there are other names or variations of these. If one day that man from outer space does visit the United States and is told that these organizations and hundreds more are really all the same thing, he may well ask, "Why so many different names?"

We could only tell him that lack of a standard name gives some indication of the complex and sometimes rather aimless development of the American community theatre. And yet in a few brief decades this important national expression has grown until today it does most of our country's play production.

This has happened with an idea which grew without precedent, has not yet developed a format, and has seen the central reason for its existence change direction no less than four times. That it *has* happened is one more testimonial to the American's amazing range of abilities and to one of his twentieth-century adventures: testing his strength in cultural areas.

There were some early prophets of the community theatre, the wisest perhaps being Percy MacKaye. In 1909 he wrote his dream of a new kind of theatre: "There is participation, there is creative expression, there is neighborly ritual." This found few understanding readers at the time, since the American theatre was rich and successful, enjoying the kind of esteem we proffer any going industry. Had we told the Shubert brothers in 1912 that they were really working in an art form, they would have smiled as they paused on their way to the bank. Had we gone on to forecast that by mid-century most American play production would be in the hands of the volunteer worker, they would, I am sure, have burst out laughing.

Yet it has happened; that theatre has come into being; that theatre which Mr. MacKaye wrote so long ago "should be dedicated to public, not private, ends."

Prophets do not often win a wide, believing audience when they first state their credos, so that we cannot be certain how closely the early community theatres were following Mr. MacKaye's text; but we do know that there was a related, almost unstated, feeling of protest in the first organizations. A number of college societies had worked at theatre, principally in New England, but as a starting point in the story of community theatre it seems well to take the date 1912, and two of the organizations which began that year.

Maurice Browne's ninety-nine-seat Chicago Little theatre and the Toy Theatre of Boston, not worrying, I am certain, about their place in history, had an immediate and attractive mission: to bring the principles of the European Art Theatre to America. Here was cause for action: to establish on this side of the Atlantic the ideas, and resultant beauties, of Antoine, Meyerhold, Appia, Stanislavsky, and the others.

Broadway, the two thousand stock companies, and the road had no time for such nonsense—yet. Business was too good. The bright tapestry of the European Art Theatre idea found another audience, one which had the time and means for developing theatre groups. The women's clubs were the logical backers for such projects and in many cities the history of the community theatre goes back to the day when the club did a one-act play, written, of course, by Synge, Shaw, Yeats, or Lady Gregory.

It is from this period that we inherit the adjective "little" found in so many community theatre names today. Most of the elements in these theatre groups before 1920 were "little": little audiences, little plays, little trained leadership—but they were dealing with some big ideas. So potent were the principles of the European Art Theatre that by 1920 they moved right from the little theatres to Broadway. In some cases the transition was complete, as the Provincetown Players, the Washington Square Players, and others became commercial ventures.

Momentarily, it looked in the early twenties as if the little theatres could call it a day with mission accomplished. They had fought for finer artistic principles in the American theatre and they had won; showbusiness was using them on almost every opportunity. If Broadway was all going to be like the early great successes of the Theatre Guild, what place was there now for the volunteer theatre?

Before many community theatres knew they needed a new reason for existence, the reason was found—and it wasn't completely new. It went back to those first one-act productions when the little theatres introduced many of the best European plays to American audiences. Typical of the exciting premières which often went almost unnoticed, the Little Theatre of Duluth in 1914 began its career with the American première of *Dark Lady of the Sonnets*.

Yes, the little theatres had been kind to new playwrights, and in the 1920s the new play and the new playwright gave the community theatres valid reason for continuance. Here in the low-budget field of community theatre might be the Golden Gateway for the New Playwright. In 1925 it was getting expensive to do a play on Broadway!

Again there is an interesting correlation between the objective of the community theatres and its effect on showbusiness. New scripts, the art play, and a smattering of classics made up a large part of community theatre programming from 1920 to 1930. There wasn't much point in doing the Broadway successes since the stock and road companies were busy at the task in thousands of theatres from coast to coast.

Not all the new playwrights fulfilled their promise, but in a number of cases the early works of some of our greatest dramatists were done in the simple facilities of a little theatre. Again Broadway looked and learned. Once a playwright began to produce good work, the theatres of Times Square were his. One of the quickest trips from obscurity to fame was, of course, made by Eugene O'Neill. One afternoon Robert Edmond Jones was arranging the furniture on Susan Glaspell's front porch in Provincetown for the staging of an O'Neill one-act, and then suddenly it was 1921 and O'Neill had won the Pulitzer Prize with *Beyond the Horizon*.

This acceptability of the new playwright by Broadway tended not only to accelerate but also to monopolize. The fine flowering of fresh talent—Barry, Sherwood, Howard, Rice, Kelly, Anderson, and the others—lifted tremendously the quality of work done on Broadway. There was a subtler, but important, effect in this welcoming of new dramatists to the market place. The young writers now became reluctant to have their work done anywhere else. Why risk a community theatre production when the new script might be done on Broadway?

1929 gave promise of being the best year showbusiness had ever known. Technically, it was using the full potentials of the European Art Theatre. For material it had the work of the rapidly maturing group of playwrights who had been so recently called "new." Financially, the future had never looked better. Added to the riches of the Broadway run, the revenues of the road and the stock rights was Hollywood's new gadget, the talking picture. Already astronomical figures were being bandied about Sardi's as amounts being offered for screen rights to the hit plays. It was exciting. It was great. It was almost too good to be true.

Then came the depression.

In a shockingly short space, the glittering empire of show-business almost disappeared. The stock companies closed, the road ceased to exist, and Broadway glumly tightened its belt and wondered if next season would be better.

As the dust of the debacle slowly settled, some observers were startled to notice that there were still curtains going up across America. The community theatres, almost forgotten in the last, lush days of the boom, were still there. For those of us who were seeing that those curtains went up as announced, it was warming to see towns and cities suddenly discovering that theatre wasn't dead; that living theatre, their own theatre, was theirs for the making—and the taking.

Today we consider with seriousness the problem of sensible use of the increased leisure brought by our technological advancements. In the early 1930s much of our populace had increased leisure not of their choosing. For many the community theatre provided a haven where useful work could be done; tasks which helped the worker through some of the depression's dark days; and work which helped make theatre.

This widening participation because of the need to fill empty hours had an effect on community theatre purpose which did not appear fully for another decade. In the early thirties there was too much confusion, too much despair to bring a quick statement of the new reason for the existence of community theatre. I heard it first in Washington.

After our second season at the Duluth Playhouse, we took a summer cruise from California to New York through the Panama Canal. It was 1935 and we had begun to hear much of the new Federal Theatre. One lovely afternoon in the Carribean we decided that somewhere in the Federal Theatre plan should be recognition of the need for new theatre housing across the land. We felt that if these vast federal funds could leave a bit of permanent gain for the American theatre it would mean much in the better days that were surely ahead.

After we landed in New York we proceeded to Washington and the great MacLean mansion which then housed the Federal Theatre. Entering we found that every movable vestige of the past grandeur had been carted away, and the desks of the new bureau were scattered rather aimlessly through the great rooms. It gave us a strange feeling to see an oak desk, an adding machine, and a stenographer grouped before a priceless carved mantle.

At last we came to an anteroom which served as Miss Hallie Flanagan's outer office. That was as far as we ever got. When her bright young assistant learned that we were in community theatre, she knew that Miss Flanagan was too busy to see us. As she pried from us that we wanted to suggest that perhaps $2 or $3 million of the Federal Theatre funds might go into building theatres in cities which needed them, that was the end. We tried to say that at 1935 building prices presentable theatres could be built in Des Moines or Oklahoma City for $100,000 each. Thirty of these structures across the nation would give the theatre something to come back to, and meantime they could be used as community theatres.

That was it. As we were ushered quickly to the door, the bright young thing summed it up. "Federal Theatre is strictly for the relief of the actors and technicians. The community theatre will have to find its own housing. After all, it is but a substitute until the commercial theatre gets back on its feet."

A substitute! Though we did not realize it on the way to Washington's Union Station, we had heard the first phrasing of the new reason for community theatre's continuance.

Twenty-two years later the best new idea for relief and de-centralization of the commercial theatre, ANTA's Forty Theatre Circuit Plan, faces as one of its most difficult problems the lack of theatre buildings across the nation.

So the Federal Theatre's $23 million was spent with nothing to show today for the money. We still wish the thirty theatres had been built.

In October we began our third year at the Duluth Play-house, not often thinking that we were engaged in some substitute form of endeavor but rather trying our best to keep living theatre alive and taking pride in the hundreds of our colleagues who were doing the same in community theatres everywhere.

The depression decade had so many effects on the American Theatre that only now are some becoming apparent. From 1930 to 1940 the community theatre gained a hard core of strength and enlarged its meaning for so many communities that it led to the fourth, and current, *raison d'être* which has continued for more than fifteen years. And those ten years did something to the commercial theatre so that today, in the time of our greatest prosperity, showbusiness continues to consist principally of the diminishing group of playhouses around Times Square. Each year the number drops: thirty-one, thirty, twenty-nine. Observing, one gets the feeling that a great force, a noble talent, is slowly but inevitably sinking deeper into a quicksand of impossible economics. Even the splendid Lincoln Square project will not alter the basic problem on Manhattan Island.

Why should commercial theatre, once a great and prosperous industry, existing in a nation with a talent for business never known before in history, be unable to find its way back to prosperity? Why should most American theatre production be today in the hands of the volunteer?

The reasons are many. They are a blend of the original torchbearing for the principles of the European Art Theatre; the encouragement given the new playwrights; the substitute for showbusiness, and one more. Since 1940 the community theatre has satisfied a crystallized American desire for creative group action. Today a vast number of our citizens enjoy and want the experience of making theatre and serving it as audience. The longer they do it the better it is done, and the better it is done, the more they enjoy and want it.

If the average man has now become so familiar with theatre and wants it in his life pattern, why isn't he content to step aside and let showbusiness provide him with all the theatre he can take? Why aren't the Shuberts and the Theatre Guild setting up hundreds of playhouses at the same rate that every city is now getting branch banks and shopping centers? Why doesn't showbusiness again become big business?

The answer is importantly connected with the average man and his attitude toward theatre, especially community theatre. Let us look at that average man and that attitude.

Fifty years ago, theatremaking and theatre people were outside the usual range of the average man's experience. Oh yes, he went to theatre and it was not hard to find; right over there at the local Opera House. And he read of theatre people: the Drews, the Modjeska's, the Barrymores, and the Bernhardt's. The world behind that asbestos curtain, however, was cloaked in a fine, intriguing mystery. The news which seeped through at times led the average man and his family to think that people of the theatre were super beings, holding all beauties and graces. Often the opposite appraisal held: theatre folk were really social outcasts and Heaven help the family which raised an actor or actress!

That naughty purple aura which was imposed on the theatre of 1906 was chiefly the result of a nation's need for harmless excitement. There was no radio, no talking pictures, no television. There was no other source which could supply the titillating small talk which the average man needs to round out his pleasure. This social wall, though largely imaginary, was built so strongly around theatre that it took long years before the average man could realize that a talent in one of the many facets of theatre was no stranger or more immoral than a talent for playing baseball, golf, or the cello.

Looking back a half century, I have used the male citizen as protagonist with definite purpose. Although it is largely forgotten now, it was the husband and father of that day who made most of the decisions and statements about social standards. As the average woman began to assume her proper position of equality it was natural that she should, with her sharper sensitivity, be the first to respond to a new form of theatre activity.

Beginning in 1912 the early community theatre projects were chiefly executed by the energy, and powers of pursuasion, of women. I have used the term "women's clubs" to encompass the valiant efforts of the ladies of that day. As veteran theatre goers will recall, many of George Kelly's best comic points in his acidly written *The Torchbearers* were concerned with poor males bludgeoned into theatrical endeavors by their wives. We now know that this little play did untold damage to the young and struggling community theatre idea.

But the idea met and overcame much bigger obstacles in

the early years, and one of the most difficult was changing the average man's attitude. As his family, and some of his friends, began to work at play production in the 1920s, he found his viewpoint changing often. Hearing reports of a production in which a member of his family was participating, and then seeing a reasonably good performance, he tended to think that there was definite merit in the procedure and that theatre was not meant to live in a purple aura.

About that time some player, usually in Hollywood, would do something to offend the social code and the resultant commotion would make the average man think that Grandfather was right: theatre was wicked *per se*. It is unfortunate that any untoward action of a theatre person becomes front-page news. Our communication marvels seem to take a special delight in over-emphasizing some poor player's misstep. This is chiefly true of Hollywood people and, in most cases, involves persons of small talent whose only claim to importance is that they have once been in a movie, or that they live in Hollywood.

It was this tendency to lump all fields of entertainment into one heterogeneous mass which made it hard for the average man to bring himself into active participation with an enterprise which bore the name "theatre," although it was preceded by "community."

There were other factors which delayed and lengthened the time it took to build a new and rational attitude toward community theatre. Two terms which upset the average man as he began to understand, were "amateur" and "amateur theatricals." Of course there have been horrible crimes committed in the name of theatre by the inept, the untalented, the misguided. Many of these were done in the oft-maligned name of sweet charity: from the high school play done solely to raise money for new band uniforms to the lodge minstrel show "put on" to secure funds for repainting the hall.

Certainly there were times, and there were communities, which rightly feared the havoc which might be wrought by the "amateur" actor. Today, in most localities, understanding has come that it is not the factor of pay which makes an actor good or bad, but how talented he is and how he is trained. Americans have always held the amateur sportsman in high esteem, and "professional" applied to an athlete still gives a deflating business overtone to the whole affair. Perhaps the group attitude is typical in football. I have yet to see a crowd watching the most expert of the professional teams evidence half the spirit and outward appearance of pleasure which you can find at almost any college stadium on a Saturday afternoon in the Fall.

With the amateur athlete there is a wide range of performance levels. A town baseball team or a high school football team with a paucity of good players and an inadequate coach can and often does give a bad performance. Yet upon leaving the game I do not recall hearing anyone say with scorn, "amateur athletes," although that night after the high school play you may well hear disparaging remarks about "amateur theatricals."

The years have gone, but the years have built, and today we find the average man with a viewpoint about community theatre which is, on the whole, sound and reasonably accurate. In many cities the playhouses are now in their middle and late thirties, and the good they have done is cumulative. In these cities the normal attitude of the citizen who has never belonged to the community theatre is that he thinks it fine, he hears the plays are good, and in general it has the same approval which he gives to the library, the symphony, and the art gallery.

There is an interesting recent tendency for the citizen to

favor his city's community theatre when it is discussed in relation to the commercial theatre. A standard remark is, "I saw the play in New York, and then again when our theatre did it, and I really enjoyed it more here." The gentleman who speaks in this fashion is often one of the great majority who participate in their community theatres only as members of the audience. He is not thinking of the Chamber of Commerce when he makes the statement; rather he is expressing normal local pride in a civic asset.

His comparison with Broadway is not our point at the moment, although he may have had justification for the evaluation which we shall consider later.

What matters here is the tremendous distance the average man has come in his attitude toward community theatre. That it has happened is of great importance to community theatre today and tomorrow. The United States is first of all a nation of businessmen, the most capable ever known. As a result of their skill, we have come to know a standard of living which is the envy of the world. But living on our standards would be an empty experience had we no achievements in the arts.

Today we have them. Our symphonies, our civic opera companies, our galleries all attest to the talent and wealth of our land. For the average man these are chiefly spectator areas; he can enjoy but he cannot do. It is in theatre that our citizens have found the widest and most satisfactory expression. No longer a distant world peopled by glamorous and mysterious players, theatre in the United States reflects the abilities and the imaginations of the town or city. It is people working at the play. It is theatre of the community.

CHAPTER TWO

The Organization of a
Community Theatre

If you were to ask a founder of New Orlean's Le Petit Théâtre du Vieux Carré or the Des Moines Community Playhouse, "How did your theatre begin?" you would probably get similar answers. Looking back over thirty-seven or eight years the founder would probably say, "A small group met and decided to do a play." If you were to ask them or founders of the other older community theatres, "What were your objectives? Did you plan then to grow into a civic institution?" the answers would probably become varied, and perhaps not too accurate, as the years between would tend to color the facts.

Many group activities in our country which have grown to strength and significance were in the beginning little more than a slight manifestation of a rather vague desire. So it has been with community theatre. When Gilmor Brown did his first production in the Pasadena Woman's Club in 1917, I doubt if even he fully envisioned that the idea would grow finally into the million-dollar Pasadena Playhouse.

Today for the many community theatres which are just beginning, and for the many more which are to begin, there are similarities in the basic motives with those of our veteran playhouses when they were first established. In a good many instances there should be important differences, changes in procedure which will limit lost motion: lessons which have been learned and relearned during the devious course of the American community theatre.

The origins of new theatre groups today fall into three general types. First, and perhaps still the most frequent, is the coming together of persons who "want to do a play." I like to feel that in most of today's situations the phrase is more accurately expressive when it reads, "want to start a theatre." That difference is important, and surely justified, after our nearly half-century of community theatre growth.

Second, and comparatively new, is the community theatre which begins as part of a city's recreation department program. This is an interesting development which has attained real success in certain instances.

The third usual beginning comes with a director, often young, who wants a theatre and can attain one only by creating an organization. With the more precise training of directors for community theatre, this type of origin is becoming more common and sometimes results in successful organizations in communities which had previously been devoid of living theatre.

All of these have common problems and pitfalls, most of which can be avoided by taking advantage of lessons bitterly learned in the past. There is a fourth, and not too uncommon, group concerned with organization, and that is the theatre which is "starting over." There are cities which have had four or five community theatres in succession with varying fallow spaces between. They need especially to be concerned with proper organizational procedure so that this time they will continue.

There are several questions to be answered at the start by each of these four general groups. First, "Does the community need this theatre?" For a town or city with no previous record of community theatre activity this question is not easy to answer. A reasonable initial step is to survey the support which the community gives to other cultural endeavors: the civic orchestra, the concert series, the civic opera or chorus, and perhaps the dramatic offerings of the local high school or college. If the record shows a reasonable, continued support for these activities, it is fair to assume that living theatre might well earn the same. If the town has shown no interest in any other of the lively arts, it might be presumptuous to assume that the stage could find followers.

This guaging of the level of belief in the arts is a fundamental element in the decision to start a theatre and more important than per capita income or the average educational level. Population is not too important a factor, except that in very small towns there is an obvious limit to the future size of the project. An outstanding example of a state which has developed community theatre in small population centers is Wisconsin. Due to the years of excellent work by the Wisconsin Idea Theatre, Wisconsin towns of twelve to fourteen hundred have thriving community theatre programs.

There is a rather infrequent variation of the beginning group which should nevertheless be particularly honest in answering the question as to whether the community needs a new theatre: this is the splinter group, which forms when a number of persons decide to pull away from an established theatre and start their own. These groups are generally composed of people who would rather run something, even badly, than be subordinate parts of a larger organization. This happens most frequently in the large cities and, from the record of the years, such a splinter group seldom amounts to much unless it happens to be answering an honest need for another theatre.

Assuming that our various hypothetical groups have decided that the new theatre is needed, a second question awaits consideration. "Is the interested group representative of the community?" This needs an honest, objective answer. Quite normally the first impetus toward organization tends to be among friends or at least acquaintances. Here is where another good look at the town must be taken. If there are two or three large industries, there should be representative persons from those industries involved in the organization of the new theatre. Are there people from the college, the communication media, the teachers, the literary clubs, and the other social groups, that should be interested in living theatre? I doubt if any community theatre ever had 100 per cent representation in the beginning. What is important is the desire for that representation and continued efforts to get it.

The recreation department as a source of theatre starts off with the comfortable stability of association with an established civic program, but it faces other problems. The chief problem is that the majority of those first involved are young people and the transition to a broadly encompassing age group is not easy. That it has worked in such cities as Milwaukee and Santa Barbara should suggest exploration of the idea in other localities. In both cities mentioned there have been years of success with excellent professional directors and fine civic satisfaction with the record.

This path toward stability is also possible in those towns which have had a succession of organizations. I know of one town with such a record which is now exploring the possibility of affiliating its latest community theatre group with the recreation program and, if it happens, permanence is more than likely.

For the director who wants a theatre and chooses a community for its establishment, the representative group is essential. If he comes as a stranger, he has a difficult task ahead. He, also, must seek out representatives of the various social and business elements and sell them on his ideas and his plan. If he cannot do this, it is doubtful if he can build the kind of organization which will continue to sell itself to the community.

Once the decision to organize has been made, it is time to think of adopting a constitution. The simpler the constitution, the better if will serve.

This brief outline could be varied to fit most situations.

CONSTITUTION OF THE COMMUNITY THEATRE OF ———

ARTICLE I: NAME

The name of this organization shall be: THE COMMUNITY THEATRE OF ———.

ARTICLE II: PURPOSE

The production of living theatre for the entertainment and edification of our city, state, and region.

ARTICLE III: INCORPORATION

THE COMMUNITY THEATRE OF ——— shall be incorporated as a nonprofit educational institution under the laws of our state.

ARTICLE IV: THE BOARD

The policies and financial obligations of this theatre shall be supervised by a board of directors. They shall be fifteen in number, one-third being elected by the membership each year for a three-year term. At the first election the length of terms shall be determined by lot. No member of the board may serve more than two consecutive terms. The board will be comprised of eight men and seven women.

ARTICLE V: THE DIRECTOR

A professional director, when employed by the board, shall have complete supervision over all production factors of the theatre except in play selection, which shall be a joint responsibility of the board and the director.

ARTICLE VI: MEMBERSHIP

Anyone who pays the annual membership fee shall be a member of this theatre with full rights and voting privileges. The amount of the fee, and the number of admissions inherent, shall be determined by the board. The board may establish further classes of membership at higher fees, such as patron members, at its discretion. Such other classes of members shall have no privileges other than those enjoyed by regular members.

ARTICLE VII: OTHER EMPLOYEES

The board may hire other employees, but those whose chief duties are in play production shall be under the supervision of the director.

ARTICLE VIII: ANNUAL MEETING

An annual business meeting of the membership shall be called each year by the board with written notice going to the members one week before said meeting. Each paid member shall be entitled to vote for board members and on other motions projected at the meeting. The nominating committee to present nominations for the board shall consist of two board members and one representative from the membership. This shall prevail after the first election.

ARTICLE IX: THE OFFICERS

The officers of the board shall be elected by the board at their first meeting after the annual meeting. The nominating committee shall consist of three members of the board. The officers who shall serve for a term of one year shall perform the duties of their respective offices for the best interests of the theatre. They shall be: president, vice-president, secretary, and treasurer.

ARTICLE X: COMMITTEES

Committees of the theatre, not connected with production of the play, shall be appointed by the president. Their appointments shall coincide with the president's year in office.

ARTICLE XI: PROPERTY

All real estate, buildings, and furnishings and equipment therein shall belong on a per capita basis to the current paid-up members of this organization.

ARTICLE XII: AMENDMENTS

This constitution may be amended by a two-thirds vote of paid members who are present at the annual meeting. All amendments must be submitted to the membership in writing one week before the annual meeting.

The two principles of the constitution are clear: first, the setting up of a functional, democratic, one-class organization, and second, the definition of the area of work for the director and any other professional employees so that they may have freedom to work under a board-defined general policy.

For the many community theatres which still operate with volunteer directors it may be necessary to qualify some of the conditions, but it is wise for them to assume that they will one day mature to professional direction.

By-laws will vary according to local situations but they should be kept at a minimum.

I cannot state too strongly my faith in the small, rotating board. Most playhouses which operate with boards numbering more than fifteen find them unwieldy and have set up an executive committee to do most of the actual work.

The relaxed way in which the community theatre idea has grown is illustrated by the wide variance in membership plans. These range from the scrip-book system, where an entire season's admissions may be used for one play, to the closed membership plan, which allows but one admission to each member for each production.

Between these are others, such as the regular open membership where cash tickets are sold to anyone as space permits. There is also the rare, and antiquated, system where a "membership" is sold for a dollar or so and then the "member" pays a seat charge for each production he attends.

Each plan has its proponents. The goal of the scrip-book system is, of course, that the members will enthusiastically use up their books before the season is over and buy a second. That is a worthy ambition, but groups operating under this plan complain rather consistently in their programs that the members tend to put off using the coupons regularly and that the final production of the season cannot take care of the patrons.

The scrip-book also fails to assure a regular audience for each play and tends to put undue emphasis on the production of "sure box-office" plays. Except that the money is in the bank, the scrip-book plan, as related to audience size, has the same faults that come with operating a theatre with only a straight box-office sale.

The closed membership which gives one admission to each play to the member is, I think, a definite improvement. The continuing audience is one of the basic tenets of community theatre. Once established, the playhouse has a freedom in program building not possible under the straight box-office plan. This is not in opposition to any part of showbusiness philosophy, although it is the antithesis of the old stock company "come to the show next week" sales pitch. In fact, one of the longest consistently fine production records of the commercial theatre was made under the Theatre Guild Subscription Plan, in effect a closed membership.

The sale of cash tickets with the open membership plan has both merit and fault. The revenue, especially with a hit, is pleasant. And there are those who say it is good to try to make every play please. If they mean to please the nonmember to the extent that he will buy a cash ticket, I disagree. Once you begin to depend on the casual attender, the one who "will come when there's one I want to see," for either approval or revenue, you are enmeshed in the worst faults of show-business.

Young theatres and young directors seldom realize that the most vocal of their patrons are usually more interested in their own importance than in any part of a theatre's good. The great majority of a community theatre audience is a quiet, interested entity which will show its approval in the most important way—by buying memberships for the next season. If you have to depend on the casual ticket-buyer, your situation is not safe or happy, for he does not trust your theatre, or your taste, or your ability, enough to buy a season ticket and try the whole season.

To emphasize the point that your playhouse works first for its membership, make certain that the price of cash tickets is well above the per-play membership rate. If the season ticket gives five plays for $7, or at a rate of $1.40 per play, be certain that the cash tickets are at least $2. This will tend to win over the casual playgoer to membership.

Membership is one of the important foundation stones of community theatre. If a community theatre is to thrive and grow with proper respect for its heritage, there must be a continuing audience, and I know of no better way of achieving it than a membership plan which assures an audience for each play, and puts an economic reward in the hands of the member.

It is true that growth beyond a certain point makes this kind of membership less important. The Pasadena and Cleveland playhouses have worked out systems which are right for their expensively and commercially involved operations. The Pittsburgh Playhouse has grown to the point where membership revenue is perhaps less than that from straight box-office. Our discussion is not for these, but for the great majority of community theatres for whom membership supplies the economic life blood.

The Shreveport Little Theatre began the closed membership plan in 1952. With us it came about simply: the demand for memberships gave us capacity audiences for as long as it seemed feasible to run. At that point each year we close our membership and begin waiting-lists for the next season. Our audience is assured and we have no box-office sale. There is also the financial comfort of money in the bank for the year's expenses before the season begins.

This did not come quickly: the Shreveport Little Theatre operated twenty-nine years on the open membership plan. Le Petit Théâtre du Vieux Carré in New Orleans and many others use the closed membership with success. Certainly it creates a climate in which theatre of high standard and wide variety can grow. There are those who say it is wrong to shut people off from theatre. We do not shut them out. With the present transitory tendency in population, each membership renewal period, which comes in the Spring, finds 15 to 20 per cent of the memberships open. The waiting list has never filled this quota, so that there is a period each summer when new members are sought. Once a member, the individual has only to pay his annual fee to remain in the organization. There are those who would like to come to our theatre occasionally to see such items as *The Solid Gold Cadillac* and *The Desperate Hours*. I would not trade that extra bit of revenue for the privilege of scheduling *The Cocktail Party*, *Death of a Salesman*, or an original.

The membership campaign is organized like any other civic selling campaign. Some playhouses turn this important work over to committees which are too small; the larger the

THIRTY-FIFTH SEASON

{ I subscribe to the following memberships
in the Little Theatre of Shreveport for the
Season of 1956-57. Payment of eight dollars
for each membership is herewith attached. }

Names_____

Address_____

City_____

Telephone_____Signed_____

Fig. 1

number of workers, the larger the return. We have found
that the average return is about ten new memberships per
worker. In some organizations a prize membership system

THIRTY-FIFTH SEASON

DATE_____1956

RECEIVED FROM_____

$_____IN PAYMENT OF_____MEMBERSHIPS

IN THE LITTLE THEATRE OF SHREVEPORT FOR THE

SEASON OF 1956 - 1957.

_____

REPRESENTATIVE

(IF THE MEMBERSHIP IS ONLY HALF PAID, IT IS UNDERSTOOD THAT THE SECOND HALF
IS TO BE PAID BEFORE SECURING TICKETS FOR THE SECOND PLAY.).

Fig. 2

is widely used. For each ten new memberships brought in, the worker receives a free prize membership. Some committee members will earn two or three, while others do not reach the quota, but it is reasonable to count on an average of ten per worker. In our organization anyone who did not belong during the current season is considered a new member.

There are playhouses which give workers credit for bringing in renewals, but we have found that unnecessary. At the fifth production of our six-play season we begin our re-newal campaign. The editorial page of the *Playbill* carries a message on the importance of prompt renewal. The card in Fig. 1 is enclosed in the Playbill, and between the acts mem-

FIG. 3

bership committee members are on duty in the foyer to receive the cards and checks. These cards, together with the receipt form in Fig. 2, are later used by the committee when they solicit new members.

A useful item for the membership committee is the annual calendar (Fig. 3) that we have used for a number of years. Giving all dates for the Playhouse season, it also carries valuable membership and box-office facts on the back. A printing firm gives us five thousand of these each year for the small ad which appears on the back.

In June and August the old members who have not yet renewed are sent statements. By September the membership is usually complete and the members are sent calendars and

		MEMBERSHIP RECORD		LITTLE THEATRE OF SHREVEPORT			
SEASON	DUES PAID	DATE	BALANCE	DUES PAID		DATE	BALANCE
19 55-56	8 00	9/13/55	-				
19 56-57	8 00	9/7/ 56	-				
19							
19							
19							

	ATTENDANCE RECORD						
SEASON	SHOW NO. 1	SHOW NO. 2	SHOW NO. 3	SHOW NO. 4	SHOW NO. 5	SHOW NO. 6	SHOW NO. 7
19 55-56	✓	✓	✓	✓	✓	✓	
19 56-57	✓	✓	✓	✓	✓	✓	
19							
19							
19							

REMARKS

NAME: NEVLIPS, GEORGE   1909 Main Street   7-4924

FIG. 4

small identification cards to carry in their wallets. The actual membership card (Fig. 4) is kept on file in the box-office. When the member makes reservation, in person or by phone, the card is checked for the proper night. The member is unable to lose or forget his membership and the card is good for five years on each side.

A question which recurs with every beginning community theatre is, "How ambitious should our program be?" Before we can answer it intelligently we need to look at theatre's place, or lack of place, in the American community.

CHAPTER THREE

The Acceptability of Theatre in the American Community

Among the more obvious, but perhaps questionable, achievements of the twentieth century has been man's success in hurling himself across the countryside and through the air at constantly increasing rates of speed. It has had a certain numbing effect. We receive the news that a supersonic jet plane can travel a thousand, twelve hundred or fifteen hundred miles an hour with far less impact than did those Americans who first heard that an automobile had reached a speed of fifty miles per hour. This age of speed has created a far different emotional climate than that prevailing when Ethel Barrymore was starring in *Captain Jinks of the Horse Marines*. Distance has almost ceased to be a factor in our land.

This elimination of time as a factor in reaching distant places, of at last seeing the long-imagined dream, has a tendency to short-circuit the imagination. Our own planet has become almost too small for interest and even the less scholarly of the college sophomores talk calmly of interplanetary travel.

The effect of this last half century upon the community has been likewise tremendous. The restlessness attached to the boom spirit makes the ordinary citizen talk endlessly not of the quality of his town but only of how rapidly it is increasing in size. Our lives have become so gadget-filled that for some a day's routine is chiefly pushing buttons and setting dials. We are inventing ourselves out of the work we used to know, and according to eminent technologists, industry will soon be chiefly concerned in making machines to supervise machines and man will have little left but to watch them work.

Has this so changed man and his community that the very human art of theatre will drift toward unimportance, or are we almost around a long circle and nearing the point where realization of true values will again be the rule?

In the first decade of this century, theatre's place in the community and the nation was large. There was scarcely a small town whose opera house did not get a lengthy season of touring attractions. Looking back, even those who were adults at the time have difficulty realizing that then there was no radio, no television, and only a few flickering foreshadowings of the motion picture to be found in the nickelodeons.

Save for picnics and band concerts, theatre was the chief form of community entertainment. In the larger towns the stock companies flourished by the hundreds and the adoration in which the leading actors were held equalled that which is now spread over movie stars, TV comics, and hillbilly singers. Much of that theatre was not good, but it was played for a public which had a naïve set of theatre standards. The audiences came to believe, to enjoy, and to remember.

The United States had not yet become sports conscious. Golf was still a strange game played by a few of the wealthy, and the shapes of ladies' bathing suits were a somber indication that we were not yet in the age of sports. The happiest place where the community could meet for entertainment was at the theatre, where the fun was even keener in the peanut gallery than in the red plush boxes downstairs. Today we are impressed if a hit runs a full year in New York, but in those peaceful days a single play, or even a character, had a certain immortality as James O'Neill's Monte Cristo and Joe Jefferson's Rip Van Winkle played on for years.

I doubt if our world will again know a time when theatre has such domination over an American's entertainment hours. Indeed had play production not progressed beyond its simple ways of 1910 it might well have disappeared from our scene. It was geared to its audience; an audience of simple tastes, an almost Pilgrim-like morality, and no educational background in the form.

A college president of that day would not have believed that a half century later more than a thousand institutions of higher learning would be giving academic attention and dignified curriculum position to the study of theatre. Recovering from his first shock at the idea, the learned gentleman would have smoothed his Van Dyke and stated that such a thought was not only fantastic but probably immoral. About the land there are still documents which state that "this college auditorium shall be so constructed that no form of stage play or presentation shall be possible thereon." I know a few colleagues who are still struggling to do theatre in those auditoria!

But theatre did come into the educational pattern of our nation and the circumstance has had a tremendous importance to the theatre today. Like many important social phenomena, the advent was unpretentious and almost unnoticed. There had been a few dramatic clubs in the colleges but they were regarded as strictly extracurricular activities of rather less importance than the tennis team. About 1915 George Pierce Baker's 47 Workshop at Harvard began to attract attention because of the benign destiny which brought together a great teacher and students of great talent. At the same time Carnegie Institute of Technology set up some courses in theatre practice, but this was regarded as a radical project of limited tenure.

In the 1920s the spark became a flame and in respectable colleges and universities there began to appear courses in theatre. At first they were carefully camouflaged by the façade of the new speech departments. Administrators and trustees grudgingly admitted courses in speech as perhaps having some general value, but there were courageous men in the field and they brought about the amazing development of educational theatre barely in time for the coming needs of community theatre.

Professor E. C. Mabie's record at Iowa University is an outstanding example of the sudden burgeoning of academic theatre in the 1920s. Joining Professor Merrie's one-man, two-year-old department of speech at Iowa in 1921, Mr. Mabie at once set out to create living room for his ideas on theatre. In 1926 he founded the University Theatre which had for its physical plant an impossible semicircular stage in MacBride Hall. Margaret and I were in the first group of drama majors to enjoy even this much progress. I received my degree from Iowa in 1929, while she was graduated in the class of 1930.

The only access to the semicircular stage was through two three-foot doors at right and left. With no room on-stage for shifting, the problems in stagecraft were considerable. It was hard, it was wearing, but gradually we began to see that theatre, good theatre, could be made even there. Margaret and I had decided that theatre was to be our profession, but in 1929 the commercial theatre was almost overwhelming in size and apparent opportunities.

After graduation, most of our colleagues left for Broadway and Hollywood but we turned to community theatre. We wanted the privilege and stimulation of creating our own theatre, not to seek a subordinate niche in the commercial structure. In September of 1929 I became director of the

Sioux City Little Theatre and on October 5, taking a week-end away from *The Queen's Husband* rehearsals, we were married and Margaret began her career as technical director. From our first season we began to feel the impact and sense the importance of educational theatre to our work.

Slowly, and then in a steadily growing stream through the years, we were joined by those with varying amounts of experience in their college and university drama departments. As the depression deepened the stock companies died and the road disappeared, and increasing numbers of young people with majors in theatre came home from New York and Hollywood to work in their town's community theatre.

This influx of developed talents came at exactly the right time, for it meant a rapid lifting of standards—an essential condition if the volunteer theatre was to fill the void left by the collapse of showbusiness. Part of this over-all design was the fact that through the 1930s, with practically no employment possibilities in the commercial theatre, the theatre departments of the universities grew amazingly. It was as if subconsciously the nation, which had once so depended on theatre as its chief entertainment, was now developing the workers and audience through educational theatre to insure the permanence and expansion of community theatre. It is hard to see any other reason for the continued enlargement today of theatre departments across the land. The training of the teachers to teach the teachers would require far less in plants, staff, and enrollment. The job opportunities on Broadway continue to show an abysmal 90 per cent unemployed of the six thousand players *already* members of Equity; and Hollywood is no better.

Paradoxically the one field today where there is employment potential is community theatre. I use the adverb because even now we are woefully short in the specific educational elements for training community theatre leadership. There are encouraging signs here and there, but in too many institutions splendid plants and excellent faculties are still graduating theatre majors designed for employment in a kind of commercial theatre which has not existed since 1932.

A final dividend of educational theatre is the fine, broad education its graduates receive. With the gains in poise, self-confidence, appreciation, and the background of learning in general subjects as well as the arts, the drama major is well fitted for many modern vocations. Further, he is aesthetically well suited to rich enjoyment of the increasing leisure which seems destined in our American way of life.

The chief beneficiary of more than three decades of educational theatre is obviously the community theatre. The thousands who have been graduated with experience in drama departments have become a vast army of theatre workers and the central core of a great audience. Without this desire for the experience of theatre instilled during the impressionable college years, the noncommercial theatre today might be a tiny project. Had educational theatre not appeared at its point in time and developed so magnificently, the Genii of the Tubes might have been in complete control of the American audience during the second half of the century.

The forecasters of the theatre's demise have thus far been consistently wrong. A large volume could be made of their dismal forebodings. When D. W. Griffith began to peddle *The Birth of a Nation* in the remodeled stores which first served as movie houses, there was much wailing. "This is the end of theatre," said the savants of drama's doomsday. "How can the stage compete with the grandeur, the scope, the magnificence of the screen?"

Then came radio. After the first aesthetic orgy of tuning in the Kansas City Nighthawks and Old Man Henderson of Shreveport on the crystal sets, the soothsayers began to listen to the soap operas and renew their prophecies. "With great radio drama coming into the home, who will buy tickets to the theatre?" But though *One Man's Family* grew through several generations, and Amos and Andy are nearing the age of Social Security, more stage curtains are rising in the United States than ever before.

The purveyors of gloom were sure they had us when movies began to talk. Now at last was theatre undone! Who would go to a play when, as the great sign once said in Times Square, you can "listen to the ticking of a clock." But from *The Jazz Singer* to the latest supercolossal epic in Vista-Vision, Techni-color, 55 Cinemascope, and Stereophonic Sound, the talking picture has not moved an inch toward the real secret of theatre. As one watches the pretty murals on the wide-wide-screen, with somewhat the feeling of looking through a transom, one wonders if this is really better than the old way. Some of the wisest men in Hollywood do not think it is, and continue to win Oscars with the old-fashioned standard-screen, black-and-white movies. As George Seaton said during his term as president of the Motion Picture Academy of Arts and Sciences, "I think it is more exciting to paint a portrait than a mural."

The electronic tubes were far from through with theatre when they threw radio and talkies at the Fabulous Invalid. Coming was the real destroyer, television. Now the Gabriels really began to blow their horns. "Every home in America will become a miniature theatre; first in black and white and then in full, glorious color! When the family can have Pinky Lee, Dave Garroway, Ed Sullivan, Steve Allen, exciting drama, and even wrestling, who will leave the living room to go to theatre?"

But a talking photograph is a talking photograph whether it

is on a screen one hundred feet wide or one which measures twenty-four inches. Even the "being televised live at the moment you see it" does not change the truth, except to expose the actors who do not know their lines and to reveal the occasional mistakes of a careless cameraman.

One day we will probably have television on our living room walls, ten feet wide with three dimensions, and a full range of smells, but the Genii of the Tubes will not destroy theatre. They will be unable, like many other projections of science, to create life.

This is theatre's eternal secret, the creating of living emotional experiences by the living actor *and* the audience working together. Only in theatre is there *mutual* emotional experience. For 2500 years man has found theatre a rewarding and satisfying experience. Call it Catharsis, soul-refreshment, what you will, the fact is a truth of civilization.

To reverse the coin we might ask if this Century of Science could so change man that he would lose the desire for theatre's gift. Does man, in creating a robot-world about him, tend to become like the machinery, or does the plethora of gadgets rather tend to make him instinctively withdraw to his most human manifestations? Case in point: does the average man need theatre more or less than he did fifty years ago?

Wise architects have long known that modern design cries for the touch of nature, and plantings, pools, and open sky are used to break the cold efficiency of line and mass. Man's instinctive revolt against the machine is indicated by industry's sudden discovery of color. Already the all-white kitchen seems quaint and the do-it-yourselfers, using foolproof paints, have made the interiors of their homes gardens of color. The automobile, which so long reserved the color-punch for fire engines and ice-cream carts, now comes adorned in a spectrum glory greater than Solomon could ever have dreamed.

Beauty is essential to the average man. Paint his machines as you will, they are still machines and will not wholly satisfy his need. The great popularity of participator sports, and the turning to the out-of-doors, is further evidence that man seeks balance in the age of science. Beyond the backyard barbecue, the eighteen holes of golf, and the sailboat on the lake there is need for more intricate emotional release.

For a great many, theatre is the answer. Living through a play is about as basic and continuing an experience as we can find for our leisure. In some ways it is man at his most human. In the curvature of time, a man from Mars might view two points in time, two softly-lit stages holding performances of *Hamlet*. Would the visitor really see much difference between Burbage and his men at the Globe and Sir Lawrence Olivier and his company at the Old Vic?

If our Martian friend failed to notice the guided missiles and hydrogen bombs, he might conclude that the creatures of earth had changed little. We of the theatre might then tell him with pardonable pride, that our pursuit has not changed because it is made of basic components of creatures who are, and will have to continue to exist as, very *human* beings. They were created with souls which instinctively search for the beauty inherent in their Creator.

For the privilege of living in his chosen community, man has been known to sacrifice other basic and natural needs. The closely knit family tends to disintegrate with our current transient pattern. Neighborliness is on the wane. Is man apt one day to forget theatre? I think not, if the current trend to regard the institution as a logical part of the civic structure continues.

Towns and cities are daily discovering that their playhouses are valuable assets. This is a new concept in the viewpoint of the American community, completely different from the attitude of a town in 1920 toward its stock company. The latter was, after all, but a branch store of a great industry. Its people, its product, and its profits were not of, or for, the town.

Today many chambers of commerce give prominent position to their community theatres in their listings of civic values. The rapid development of this interest and pride in the local theatre is of great importance to community theatre. It is part of the new reason for existence and its enlargement may have important bearing on the future.

It is interesting that this new civic enthusiasm for theatre goes far beyond the members and participants of the organization. Citizens who have never been in the local playhouse now mention it with the same pride they voice for the civic orchestra, the library, the gallery, or the baseball team.

Theatre is beginning to play a part in the thinking of the business community, as well. The corporate mind which runs a great industry faces many problems. Among them is the imperative need to see that the workers are happy with their lives away from the office or plant. Modern corporations know that the proper climate for their people must include sound, constructive leisure-time activities. A logical part of this climate is theatre. Today when new plant locations are considered, there are questions asked beyond those concerned with water, power, and railroad facilities. The forward-thinking businessman today wants to know if the town considered has good schools, a civic orchestra, and a good community theatre.

There are cases where such facilities were not readily available, so industry created them. The Convair plant in Fort Worth is typical. The men at the top knew that their 25,000 employees would do better jobs with the proper interests away from work. Convair set up its own recreation department, which includes directors and theatres where plays are made by the employees for the employees.

We have come a great distance since George Kelly thought it funny for a businessman to be involved in a community theatre play!

The acceptability of theatre in the community is now beyond debate. Man's basic need for beauty, his satisfaction in a communion of emotional experience, the broad training and conditioning of so many citizens by the educational theatre, and the growing realization of the special value a playhouse can add to civic assets—all these make theatre's place, if not assured, at least implied. And we now know that for theatre the mechanical media can never be substitutive—they hold but the thin charm of convenience.

This new concept of the place and value of theatre to the town, the city, and to industry is not uniform. Its development varies widely. In many places it has hardly begun, but its existence on so wide a scale proves its validity. Those organizations which lack civic standing, those who need wider support, must ask themselves searching questions. Does our town fail to support us because we do not truly represent it? Who makes living theatre in our community?

CHAPTER FOUR

Who Makes Living Theatre in the American Community?

Granting that theatre has been part of the life experience of many Americans and that through the ages theatre has interested and attracted varying numbers of talented people, it remains important to know the background reasons for those participating in a current community theatre. If these reasons are sound, and tend to interlock throughout the group, then the total motivation, the over-all attitude will probably be right.

First we need previous experience of theatre for the group that makes it, at least in the beginning. I do not say "in" theatre, but rather "of" theatre: the experience of playgoing. If we were starting an orchestra we would hardly try to use those who not only played no instrument but had never listened to music. Luckily, community theatre has many tasks for those who play no instrument; among the important ones is that of participating as audience.

The oldest candidates for our prospective group will be those who knew as audience the commercial theatre in their community. They are the oldest since it has been a quarter century since stock and the road made significant participation possible. In the larger towns there are some who did support living theatre through the years, who came to know and want theatre as part of life. They are not easy to find, but they will tend to come to the new theatre as audience, and return if they find satisfaction.

A smaller segment of the population will be those who see something of the Broadway seasons. Some of these confine the privilege to one item, seeing each season's biggest smash-hit musical. Such specialized patrons of one division of New York theatre are not apt to have much place, or interest, in community theatre. However, those who see several plays on Broadway each year are quite certain to be drawn to the civic playhouse; and, if the quality of the work therein is sound, they may become among the most appreciative. In Shreveport for years we have found that those who visit Broadway frequently are among the most enthusiastic segments of our organization.

Important to the making of community theatre, but still smaller in number, are those who have worked in the commercial theatre but now earn their living in another vocation. They can become valuable workers once they forget the tenets of showbusiness. As they come to understand that all the joy of theatre can now be theirs without the dread of a Saturday-night closing notice, their enthusiasm grows.

Once the commercial player understands the happy situation of the noncommercial player, he is apt to be wide-eyed and jealous. In 1955-56 the Dublin Players and the ANTA Players came to Shreveport for engagements at the Women's Department Club, which is adjacent to the Playhouse. After they had inspected our plant and come to know our people, and in the case of the Dublin company watched a performance of ours, there were repeated statements by the professionals: "What lucky people. You can enjoy making theatre and not worry about eating."

A usual and fine source for community theatre players is in radio and television. Many actors of wide experience are found in local radio and television stations, and are nearly always eager to get back on stage as their schedules permit.

Greater numerically in the organizations which make living theatre in the community will be those who have known the educational theatre both as audience and participant. High school dramatic activities are sending an enlarging stream of citizens toward community theatre. The more dignified position now held by high school drama, and the high standards which generally prevail, have made high school plays of real value for players and audience. In many localities, the high school drama teacher sees to it that her best pupils work actively at the community theatre. The gain is two-fold: the playhouse gains, and the better equipped students can raise the quality of their own school productions. The modern secondary school drama teacher, product of our great system of educational theatre, is well prepared. Any time that these teachers can give to community theatre should prove of value.

Potentially still more useful to community theatre are those who have experience in college and university theatre, either as participants or audience. The high quality of current university productions, and the age bracket of college years, makes four years of such playgoing an almost certain basis for wanting continuance of it through adulthood. The vast expansion of our college population and the rapid development of the university theatres have been perhaps the two most important new factors in creating community theatre audiences.

Our great experiment in making college education an implied portion of the Bill of Rights has been good for drama. Without mass education at the university level, millions of Americans would not have had theatregoing as an exciting part of their growing up. That they have had a slightly different impression from that their parents gained from stock and road long ago is also of vital interest. Attending that campus playhouse; watching the work of their classmates; being part of a theatre devoted "to public, not private, ends" prepares the college graduate for a logical interest and place in community theatre.

This is even more true of those who participate in university dramatics by working actively on a play once or twice during the college years. Here again is the community theatre experience, scaled down in years and with many differences, but filled with the flavor and satisfaction of the adult group's actual workings. Again it tends to create a desire for redoing and, after graduation, there is community theatre where the pattern can find repetition.

Perhaps the most important single group who make living theatre in the community are those who have taken specific theatre training in college: the drama majors. The over-all result of such an education is so complete and self-enriching that many drama graduates, finding employment in that field perhaps not to their satisfaction, begin careers in other endeavors. These people are invaluable to their community theatres.

They come today, in increasing numbers, specialists in the various phases of theatre. Their developed skills can be a source of satisfaction and inspiration to others. The drama major finds equal return as he begins to work with adult colleagues of community theatre, a logical progression from the student players of his college years.

From our records at the Shreveport Little Theatre, we have found through the years that a majority of new talent, both on-stage and backstage, has come from the university source: the drama majors and the casual participants. It is not so easy to check records on incoming members who serve as audience, but the proportion is probably equally high there.

The development side-by-side of educational and community theatre is important and no accident. Their relationship is interlocking: the academic feeds audience and participants into the community which in turn sends students with dramatic interests to the campus. This academic factor is the most important in the current attitude which regards community theatre as a cultural asset, not just a place where "shows are put on." Certainly this attitude will affect not only the future of community theatre but also the necessary decentralization of showbusiness.

In building our group to make living theatre we must not forget what can be called, for want of a better name, the traveling community theatre worker. There is today a number of highly competent players and technicians whose everyday work moves them from place to place. They have found that the established community theatres are much alike and that they find theatre to do, and make friends in the doing, regardless of the city. This is particularly true of men in military service. If they like working in theatre, they can always find a home away from home at the community theatre nearest their base. For more than twenty years in Shreveport we have enjoyed the proximity of Barksdale Air Force Base. The friendship has brought us scores of talented players and technicians, an important contribution to the quality of our acting company. At installations out of the country or in remote areas, theatreminded men and women often begin their own theatre programs.

In theory we have finished "casting" our community theatre group. We have the residue audiences from the various times and phases of the commercial theatre and the ex-professionals. For players we have those actors earning livings in radio and television. Next comes the large number who have known the educational theatre at secondary and college levels as audience and casual participants. Our sequence comes then to those trained specifically for the theatre by the universities; and last, but far from least, the transient, experienced community theatre worker.

It is intriguing to notice that this building of the community theatre group on a common experience of, or in, theatre, ignores and cuts across the normal, established social strata of a town or city. This is pertinent and important and needs wide understanding. Community theatre must cut across established social lines if it is to deserve the name.

The people who write up for theatre programs those lists of professions, occupations, and crafts represented in a single cast and crew seem always surprised that a lawyer, a carpenter, a teacher, a radio announcer, a debutante, a housewife, a mechanic, a student, a doctor, and a policeman should be cast together in a play. The matter of real interest to me is that the common experience of, or in, theatre should permeate so many phases of our social structure. Once we put our attention on this common interest, the everyday titles of our people are forgotten and we think of them as players and technicians.

In the splendid democracy of the best community theatre, it is possible for the clerk to do a better job and earn better notices than the vice president of the bank. If he does, it is not because anyone has a brief *for* a clerk, or *against* a banker, but because they are being judged only on their ability to serve theatre and the play.

This miniature mirror which community theatre holds up to democracy has not always been present, and regretfully there are still organizations which reflect a single stratum of society. Forty years ago the dramatic club attitude was prevalent. It was easy to establish because it was too often assumed that this kind of theatre could begin with a group of friends. In the early years, with leisure and theatre training far less common, there were many groups which might well have been called "The Four Hundred Playhouse," and their application forms headed, "List your social standing first and then theatre qualifications—if any."

This was a logical first home for the idea, but as the idea grew and developed, the dramatic club was no longer big enough to hold it. Thus my quarrel is with those few situations about the land which, unwittingly or not, have failed to grow beyond the club philosophy and are strangling the theatre potential of their communities. At times in established playhouses I have heard otherwise sensible people say, "I didn't know a single person in the cast." The manner implied, of course, that since none of the players were fortunate enough to be a friend of the speaker, the total result could not be very good.

We are a nation of organizations and there are countless clubs, societies, lodges, and fraternities where this desire for snug, mutual acquaintance can be satisfied. Theatre is not one of these or, rather, it ought not to be.

How then can the young theatres and the beginning theatres start to build the enduring foundation which is made of the over-all theatre background and interest of a community?

The starting point is the center of all we mean by theatre: the play. It is this interest in the play, the experience of plays seen, the experience of plays done, which will be the catalyst. At first the play need not be fully produced. A number of successful organizations have spent the first months in reading plays, doing walking rehearsals, as they gradually drew in from the community a representative group. This slight delay in the first formal production often means a stronger beginning.

A series of meetings devoted to discussions of community theatre objectives and concluding with a forty-minute reading by a group which has sincerely worked on the project will give participation to many and some important indoctrination to the others.

This planning period should be well publicized and newcomers made welcome. In a few months the division of talents into players, technicians, and audience will begin to be apparent. Careful records should be kept of all who attend. Those who want to serve as audience should be listed for future memberships, and among them may be workers for the membership drive. For players and technicians, a more

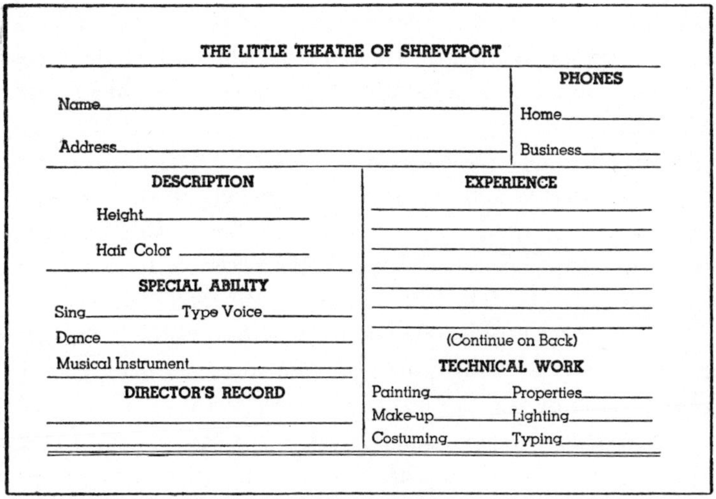

THE LITTLE THEATRE OF SHREVEPORT

Name__________ PHONES Home__________

Address__________ Business__________

DESCRIPTION

Height__________

Hair Color __________

SPECIAL ABILITY

Sing__________ Type Voice__________

Dance__________

Musical Instrument__________

DIRECTOR'S RECORD

EXPERIENCE

(Continue on Back)

TECHNICAL WORK

Painting__________ Properties__________

Make-up__________ Lighting__________

Costuming__________ Typing__________

FIG. 5

complete record is necessary. The card in Fig. 5 gives a fairly complete picture of players and crew members.

This preproduction time, this incubation period, is not an easy one. There will be those who want to get to full operation of a theatre program, those who want complete organization. My advice is to wait for both; wait until the idea of community theatre begins to draw a representative list of people together. There is danger, in crystallizing the project too early, of establishing the structure on too narrow a base. Thus it is well to delay the election of a board of directors until all the potentials for that vital place of leadership have been explored.

The beginning theatre may not be able to attract the quality of civic leaders who will later be happy to serve on the board of an established playhouse, but the best available leaders are needed. An interim committee can handle organizational matters for the first months. As capable persons are attracted, they can be added to the committee so that it becomes, in a sense, a trial board of directors. During this period the constitution can be adopted which places the machinery in readiness.

Often those who seem at first suited to board leadership reveal deficiencies and, being only members of the interim committee, they need not be inflicted on the organization for a term of board service. It is generally advisable to delay the election of the first board of directors until after the first full public production. The play will serve to intensify the interest and the drawing power of the idea and will give a fuller picture of width, and depth, of interest.

But we must not be impatient. We are not yet ready for casting and rehearsal. We are still building the foundation: trying to bring together all those with interest and experience in theatre. We will not reach them all until production begins, but the range of representation and the sincerity of effort in these formative months will do much to determine not only the future rate of progress but often, lamentably, the length of existence. When we are convinced that we have explored all potentials, gone as far as we can without full production, then we should be ready for the next step—projection of the group into action.

CHAPTER FIVE

The Community Theatre "Group" in Action

"TRYOUTS ANNOUNCED FOR FIRST PLAY."

This headline in the local press marks a significant moment for the new community theatre. The second phase of development begins with its appearance, and it brings widened community interest and new responsibilities. Now the results of the planning months will be put to test, and merits and errors will appear with regularity.

An auspicious beginning requires that the fledgling theatre has made an effort to choose a play as close to its community's center of interest as possible. It will be surprising if the organizers come close to their target, for they have had to judge the taste of their potential audience largely through the opinions expressed during the planning period.

Too often the most vocal people around a beginning theatre are apt to be wrong. Persons obsessed with having an opinion and voicing it at every possible opportunity are likely to be more interested in themselves than they could ever be in any organization. These egopinionates will not disappear as a playhouse grows older. They go on endlessly, usually in disapproval.

So the selection of the first play has been subjected to pressures by proponents of everything from *Oedipus Rex* to *Waiting for Godot*. We trust the middle-of-the-roaders have become momentarily vocal and expounded these facts: a community theatre has first to establish itself as a place where the

47

average man can find good entertainment, well executed. It is better to hit slightly below the town's cultural level than too far above it. Once an audience is built, it is possible to raise the literary quality of the program, but it is hard to induce back to a playhouse those who have been frightened away by plays above their understanding.

It is also wise to choose plays which will not risk offending the moral standards of the average man and his family. If the play contains language or situations which they find shocking, they are not likely to return. Even our "Broadway visitors" are much more lenient morally in New York than they are at home. Not many of those who saw *Cat on a Hot Tin Roof* on Broadway would want to see it scheduled for their own community theatres.

It is understood, of course, that the play selected is soundly constructed and of sufficient quality to justify the work required for its production. If these precepts have been heeded, the play chosen has a reasonable chance of pleasing, and not offending, the majority of the future audience.

From this point on, earnest efforts are made to publicize the tryouts and their importance. It must be stated in the press and on radio and television that all persons interested in play production are cordially invited to be present on the specified night. The point is underlined that the invitation includes those with interests in the various departments of production. These can be listed in the press releases: scene construction, painting, properties, costuming, lighting, and make-up.

One of the important differences between commercial and noncommercial stagecraft is that in the latter the work is done chiefly by the volunteer. Those who know the backstage climate of Broadway will appreciate this most. There the social wall between players and stagehands is so high as almost to eliminate communication between the two groups. Building the kind of team spirit common to community theatre is virtually impossible since the members of the IATSE and Equity are kept busy observing the countless union rules.

As the tryout nears, the temptation to precast is to be avoided like the plague. Maintenance of the honesty and integrity of the open tryout system has too many future values to risk impairment. It is the easy way, the lazy way, to decide that a certain talented player, or players, should have certain roles before tryouts. Organizations sometimes follow this primrose path in what they think is secrecy, but the truth will out. Perhaps a precast player will take pains to tell the secret before tryouts. The result of this practice is diminished interest and attendance at tryout sessions and soon a general public feeling that the so-called community theatre is only a dramatic club.

A more advanced stage of this condition is the system of choosing plays to fit available players. This is also tempting but dangerous and can change the expanding circle of a community theatre's work into a contracting, restricting noose. In twenty-six years, Margaret and I have never chosen a play to fit players nor have we ever precast a role. The result has been that our acting company has always been large and constantly renewed with fresh talent.

Several evils can result from making copies of the play accessible to interested players before tryouts. First, players tend to pick out their own roles. This has all the faults of any precasting plus creating an attitude in the player's mind which will make him unhappy, and perhaps unwilling, to play any role other than his chosen one.

At the Shreveport Little Theatre we seldom announce titles until shortly before the tryout date. In 1956, however, we did put into print our dates for *The Desperate Hours* six months before tryouts. The result was that a dozen or so of our best actors proceeded to cast themselves mentally in the two roles of Glenn Griffin and Dan Hilliard. At the tryouts it happened that two other actors seemed best suited for the parts and none of the precast dozen wanted to play anything else. Needless to say, we went along without them and the result was a high point of the season.

The second disadvantage of prereading of the tryout play is that it gives an unfair advantage to those who do it.

The third danger is that the individual player will begin to form an opinion and dream up an interpretation of the entire play. This is not his business; if it were, he should be at the director's desk. The individual player's chief concern should be with the part he is reading at tryouts or rehearsing later. It would seem odd if every man in the symphony had the entire score on his music stand. Good musicians would not like it; they want to concentrate on their individual parts. The interpretation, the blending, the timing, the reading—these are matters for the conductor of the symphony, and for the director in the theatre.

There is an additional, and psychologically sound, reason for the use of "sides" by the players instead of copies of the full script. From the time he is handed his individual script at tryouts until the production closes, the player concentrates upon his own assignment, his character, and lets the director blend his work into the whole. When sides are not available for rental by the playbrokers, we make our own. As the example in Fig. 6 shows, each page is a constantly growing record of the actor's progress in the role.

When the half-page sides are fastened together (oilcloth makes a durable cover) the blank page facing each typed page is used for writing out the cues. During study time, the player works on a side, then turns his script so that he can see only the written-out cues. As he answers these, he can check the ones he misses and then turn back to the typed page for further study. Use of sides greatly speeds the rate of learning and the cue page prevents any of the "cheating" that can happen when a card is used to cover speeches during study.

ACT II -7-

-----rehearsing?

Jumping out of the Embrace

Oh! How do you do, Miss Lanning. Mr. La Tour said something very nice to me.

-----I'm sure it must have been.

straighten my Hair

Yes, he was complimenting me on President Garfield.

----oh, yes, of course.

X to DLC

(There is a pause)

Well, aren't you glad about it?

------glad the studio won't have to close.

Push it

But aren't you pleased that it's such a hit?

------necessarily mean the picture's good.

Bridling

Are you insinuating anything?

----of course not.

X R 2

What is it then?

FIG. 6

Tryouts are conducted by the director with full authority. The volunteer director, judging his neighbors and friends, faces several dangers not usually present when the director is a professional who has been brought to the town. He runs the risk of being accused of partisanship, of letting friendships sway his judgment. But once having assumed the position of director, he has to do his own casting.

There are organizations where the innately personal, highly demanding process of selecting a cast is attempted by a casting committee. Nothing could be more at variance with modern theatre practice which is based on the principle of the artist-director, the mind-in-the-middle, which blends all elements of production into the image born in his imagination. Though there are many sitting in the director's chair who are far from artist-directors, yet if the play is to have a chance for life we are forced to follow the central authority principle.

The director has studied his play well, he knows the kind of personalities and types he would like in the various roles. He should begin the evening of tryouts with an open mind, avoid precasting even now. Each prospective reader should be asked to secure his file card (Fig. 5) or to fill one out. This is the permanent working record of players and crew.

I have found it best to ask the readers to keep their cards until they begin to read; the director, taking them at that time, can begin his specific notes thereon. I have also found it well to let players read more than once, often in two or three parts. This keeps a fluid quality to the procedure and does not imply any casting decisions. I always ask those interested in understudy work and crew activities to be certain we have them in mind. I have gained my first impression of many fine acting talents when I have heard the phrase, "If I do not win a part in the play, I would like an opportunity to do an understudy."

During the evening the director should halt the readings to explain that this is but the first step in casting the play. He should say that within a stated period of time he will telephone the most likely prospects for second readings, which will be private. This series of individual meetings gives the director a chance to appraise strangers, to give those who do not read well at sight a chance at now-familiar material, and often unmasks those who sounded excellent at the first reading, but whose chief talent may be glibness.

The explanation should continue to say that after the private readings, a tentative group will be called together for a reading. This is essential for a final check of voice contrasts, sizes, colorings, and a further appraisal of each player's fitness for the role and of his ultimate potential in it. Not until this second group reading is over should the director make final decisions. Naturally no players will be given scripts to take away from the playhouse until this point.

This detailed casting procedure takes time, but it is a pattern which if followed tends to result in accurate casting. Reference to the calendar in Chapter Two will show that at Shreveport three weeks elapse between our open tryouts and the first night rehearsal. This timetable has many values, among them allowing the players to adjust their personal schedules so that nothing will interfere with rehearsals.

Announcement of the rehearsal schedule should be made at the first tryout and the seriousness of meeting that schedule stressed. For twenty-five years our plan has encompassed a five-night work week, Monday through Friday, from seven-thirty until ten-thirty. Noncommercial actors, their days busy earning livings at other vocations, like definition of the time involved in doing a play, and strict adherence by the playhouse to the days and hours will build respect and conscientiousness among players and technicians.

With the first play now cast and ready to begin rehearsals, the new theatre should begin work on the second production. The preliminary steps of play selection, announcement of tryouts, and the other items involved with the first production have now to be repeated. If only three plays are to be done in a season of nine months, then it is possible to wait until a play closes before holding tryouts for the next. However, the overlapping of production details, tryouts for the second before the first opens, have an important effect.

This plan begins to emphasize the vital point that community theatre is a *continuing* process, not a series of isolated productions. This has great bearing on membership sales, program planning, and public acceptance of the idea and its place in civic life. Every effort made to build this spirit and feeling of continuity has value. In essence, the impact of one production can lead the audience to expect and want the experience again. Some organizations, among them playhouses of some years, seem to operate in a series of jerks; productions do not interlock; even performance dates are undecided until the last minute. The public senses this and sometimes fails to give such theatres credit for permanence.

While the young community theatre works to earn and receive the proper public attitude, it faces a formidable morale problem within. It is the necessity of building a team spirit from the widely varied motives and talents which have brought the group together. My acquaintances among the football coaches often intrigue me with the early season remark about their squads: "The boys have great spirit!" At times it is their chief asset, but the effort to build team spirit with football players seems simple compared to the same objective in theatre. The most self-centered halfback knows that if he does not work for the *team*, some guard or tackle may one day step aside and the halfback may have his head knocked off. But the very structure of a play and of a theatre organization tempts the egotist, the self-centered, to "steal scenes." And we must face it: individualistic extroverts often have great talent for theatre. The commercial theatre at times has seen virtuoso talents sacrificing the real point and meaning of the play for personal emphasis. This happens despite the paycheck club which hangs over their heads.

To build team spirit with volunteer players is difficult, but it has to happen if the organization is to progress. A simple signpost indicates the way: "The play must come first." This phrase should be over every community theatre stage door and in the dressing rooms, and it should be planted in the minds of the company by the director at every opportunity. This viewpoint is one of community theatre's greatest strengths.

Loss of this attitude as the primary objective is a price the commercial theatre frequently has to pay for survival. Often on Broadway the first question is not, "Is this manuscript worthy of production?" but rather, "Will it be a hit?" Translated into economic terms, the second question is, "Will it make money?" This concession has a fissionable quality. Now a star has to be hired who enjoys a great following (dollars at the box-office). This goes on until the poor play is lost and the opening night curtain may reveal a creation far removed from the playwright's dream.

Our present concern is not with Broadway's required sacrifices but with community theatre's opportunity. By keeping the play always first, we gain in many directions. Even the most self-interested players may be saved for the future if they can once try the principle and see the results. What is good for the play? The play first. The play.

Gradually the team spirit will build. Not all the egotists will be saved; a life-time habit cannot always be changed. A happy surprise for the observer is to discover the often splendid unfolding of the more latent talents, the less positive personalities. With an unselfish goal, the play as the high objective, these people often work tremendously and surprise even themselves with the result. This is a logical phenomenon, one common to the playing field. The unselfish motive, devotion to the team or the play, can make the athlete or the actor surpass himself.

It will be a few seasons before the young theatre is apt to hear, "I saw this same show on Broadway and I liked the play better here." The cynic will scoff at the thought that a New York production costing $100,000 could be compared to a community theatre offering which involved no more than the spending of $1100 or $1200, and yet the remark is often honest and accurate.

If we examine the statement we see that the speaker did not say that he thought the leading lady was better than Tallulah Bankhead or that the scenery was finer than the work of Jo Mielziner or Peter Larkin. What was said was that the spectator liked the *play* better as he lived through it at the community theatre. In this experience he had not focused his attention on one or two virtuoso talents; he had not waited impatiently while the stars were off stage; he had not seen direction which pointed up the work of the highest salaried players. He had been watching the *play*. A good community theatre production often gives a clearer, more three-dimensional impression of the *play* than we get from some commercial productions.

This is another basic influence which seems to be leading the commercial and noncommercial theatres on paths of continuing divergence. It is one of the reasons why showbusiness struggles in a narrowing morass of economic impossibilities while community theatre flourishes across the land.

Not all the civic organizations are aware of the great values to be gained by making the play the one common objective. If they could but understand that it is community theatre's finest opportunity for success and progress, the conversions would come rapidly.

It is a decision which has to be made one day; delay but

slows the rate of growth. It is a focal point in the differences between the dramatic club and the community theatre philosophies. So long as individuals remain more important than the group, so long as the group makes the play less than its chief objective, then we do not truly have a community theatre. No matter which of the many titles are used for the organization, the public will know.

A recent letter states: "Our theatre was organized in 1949. We have thirty-five active members. Of late our attendance has begun to drop. Do you suppose the public is getting tired of us?" Eight years old and still a dramatic club! Of course the public is tired of a group which differs from the 1929 stock company only in that it has perhaps twenty actors while the stock company used only a dozen.

The transition from club to civic theatre does not involve changing the constitution, the name, or other structural factors. What it does demand is sublimation of self for the good of the group, and the good of the group is holding the *play* always as the first goal.

There will be some who cannot stand to give up the prestige of being an "active" member and admit every season-ticket holder to equal rights and opportunities. Others will not be able to face the prospect of "strangers" coming to tryouts and winning parts in plays. A common feature in many of those who oppose the transition is that they hold their own importance more dear than any organization.

Sociologically, then, the formation, fusion, and transition of the community theatre group is far from an easy process. First gathered by cutting across the whole social structure of a town and assembled by the drawing power of common experience in, or of, theatre, the group presents a list of possible social and economic conflicts which may take years to adjust.

Adjustment and fusion is possible quickly, however, if based upon the original reason for gathering, the theatre. And transition from the club to the community theatre is again possible if the center of action is kept at the center of theatre —the play.

This involved set of social problems and adjustments depends for solution upon the next subject of discussion: community theatre leadership.

CHAPTER SIX

Leadership in the Community Theatre

Leadership at times gets into strange hands. This is true not only of theatre but of other group projects of mankind, such as politics. Politicians, however, regularly give the public a chance to "vote the rascals out," unless the evil grows to dictatorship which then requires extermination.

Problems in community theatre leadership do not develop to that degree but they are often complex. Minor situations are sometimes heightened by the sensitive personalities involved. Yet I do not believe that the talented people who make theatre create any greater emotional crises than those following more phlegmatic pursuits.

The distressing feature of mistakes in or by community theatre leadership is the far-reaching damage which often results. Other organizations seem more resilient in recovering from injury inflicted by poor leaders. Not so the theatre. In town after town there are stories told of a theatre which existed until a mistake was made in leadership. The record seems about evenly divided between errors by boards of directors and by hired professional directors.

Not always fatal, this type of difficulty nearly always retards and sometimes leaves a lasting blemish on an organization. When we see groups of rather impressive age still struggling to find a permanent home, to progress to the point of professional direction—still trying to solve infant problems in their adulthood—we can usually find in the case history a period of poor leadership.

Another class of difficulties is encountered by playhouses which once had professional direction but have now returned to the volunteer system. If the director left for a better position with the theatre in good health, then any retrogression can be blamed on the local citizenry. An organization which disintegrates around the paid director, however, points the finger of guilt in most cases at the professional. There are cases where the director's difficulty has not been of his own making, leaving him no choice but to depart. Many sad records are left where the so-called "director" had neither talent, temperament, nor qualification for the job.

It is a matter for wonder that the community theatre has grown so prodigiously in the United States with so little specific training for professional directors and even less for citizen leaders. In town after town organizations have begun, struggled, and often matured into important playhouses by trial and error. The time has come when we must try to save at least part of this lost motion, conserving the energies for the demanding task of making theatre.

As our hypothetical young group looks ahead it is apparent that two general types of leadership are needed: in production and all its elements and, to use an old showbusiness term, in the "front of the house." The speed of their acquisition and the quality of their endeavors will pretty well determine the rate of progress and ultimate success.

Heading the production structure is the director, volunteer or professional. Our beginning theatre, and many older ones situated in small population areas, will have to go along with the layman-director. This course has many handicaps, not the least of which is that we are asking persons often with little training to handle a highly specialized task in the realm of creative art. The happiest solution for the volunteer problem is that in which the local college or high school drama instructor can find time for directing the community project. This is rarely possible, however, because these trained people are usually more than completely occupied by the program at their own institutions.

Next best is to find a person in the community who has had directing experience although now in another vocation. Following that, the ex-professional player is a logical choice. In both these instances, however, there is a tendency to ask too much from the individual. It is not fair to expect a former professional, now putting in full days at another work, to direct a full season's plays. Such duties should be assumed by a professional.

The only sane solution to the volunteer problem is to find, or develop, a group of directors who will be physically able to assume a portion of the task each season. By intensive reading and an on-the-job learning process, it may be possible to develop three or four such volunteer directors.

The technical field nearly always proves a rich vein of talent for organizations regardless of age. Skill in many crafts can be funneled, with proper guidance, into a theatre's production stream. Ability with carpenters' tools, painters' brushes, and the electricians' connections find simple translation into stagecraft. There are many excellent books on the technical side of theatre and they should be a constantly used part of the playhouse equipment.

Creation with wood, canvas, paint, and light has less intricate problems than those involved in creating with human bodies, voices, and personalities—direction. The record would seem to bear this out. How often has it been said, "Our play wasn't so very well done but our setting was wonderful!"

I would not have any technical element of play production less competent; I want only to see direction raised to a level at least as fine. The twin objectives related to stagecraft are, first, to work for the day when a professional technical director-designer can be employed, and second, to keep the principle of wide participation in effect. The lazy way is to overwork the best of the technicians until they, like the best volunteer directors, are forced to stop taking part.

To avoid this loss and to build staff, each crew should follow the apprentice system. Thus the skilled carpenters, painters, and electricians can find and develop new craftsmen, spending some of their time as teachers. This spreads out the work so that the few do not begin to find it burdensome, and the organization becomes assured of having at all times adequate crews.

The fortunately uncommon practice of setting up a "club" feeling for the technical people has the same evils which that attitude brings to the players. It is the easy, lazy way, but it brings regrets. Perhaps the greatest danger lies in setting up a barrier between players and technicians. We know how importantly this division affects the climate of the commercial theatre. Although no union cards are involved, the menace begins once we say, "These are the actors and *these* are the crew."

It is important to maintain absolute democracy back of the curtain, as it must be kept through the entire organization. At the Shreveport Little Theatre this philosophy is so completely in control that our best players do not feel they have put in a full season unless they have done technical work on at least one production.

Of course I took my most important step toward achieving this harmony and unity when I married my designer in 1929. Through all these years Margaret has taught her technicians this democratic ideal of play production, so that each cast and crew is speedily welded into a cooperative team. Following the rule of wide participation, she uses more than a hundred individuals each season in the technical departments. A device which aids this, and has long-range value, is her system of day and night crews. High school and college students work at the Playhouse after school and on Saturdays. These teenagers are quick to learn and many of them grow up to be of great value to the Playhouse. The night crew, made up of adults, works through the entire rehearsal and production period. Their schedules are as prescribed as those of the players. We have found that giving dignity and responsibility to crew work pays well.

The more a theatre worker knows about all of play production, the better he will tend to do a particular assignment. For example, part of a player's technical equipment is the ability to do his own make-up. Thus at Shreveport make-up supervisors begin at a definite point in rehearsal to teach the full process to new actors who may need it, and to work with experienced players on the special problems required in make-up for the current character. When dress rehearsals arrive, the players do their own make-up with the supervisors standing by for any needed corrections.

This rapport between the technical and direction sides of the theatre has been a rewarding privilege. Our players rehearse in a technical atmosphere carefully planned to help them at every step. The moment the actors are ready for rehearsal properties, the crew which has been assembling the properties begins to work at each rehearsal. Handling of unusual costumes is made simple as the costume crew provides rehearsal costumes of matching size and weight early in the schedule.

Our players are always given roughed-in settings in the second rehearsal week. As these grow to completion with the play, actors are never handicapped in later rehearsals, when their full attention and energy should be given to their own creative problems, by having suddenly to learn how to use a stairway, a balcony, doors, and windows. They even have the luxury of rehearsing with the final furniture a week before opening. This also builds ease and confidence.

Because of this carefully planned, efficient timetable, we have been able, since 1939, to give our *Playbill* an almost unique feature. For that period, and covering more than a hundred productions, we have carried a picture of the play on the *Playbill* cover. It looks simple until you begin thinking through the time required for photography, engraving, and printing, and then you realize that setting, furniture, costuming, and make-up have had to be completed one week before opening. It is not a simple problem and, so far as I know, we are the only community theatre which has been able to picture the finished production consistently on the program. (Pictures of two or three characters taken against a small area are not the same as showing the entire cast and the full stage setting.)

All light cues and effects and all scene shifts are rehearsed for ten days or two weeks before dress rehearsal, under my wife's system of coordinating the directing and technical sides of production. This means that our dress rehearsals are really performances without audiences, with no new technical elements inserted to disturb the players. In those precious last hours of preparation, they are left free for complete concentration on creative acting.

Many organizations have to share housing, and then this gradual, planned technical growth is not possible. The poor players who have to face setting, furniture, lights, and make-up for the first time at dress rehearsal are working under handicaps. Yet even these conditions should not result in confusion. Thought, careful planning, technical work handled outside rehearsal hours, these will do much to give the most important element, the play, a chance to come fully to life. Bad dress rehearsals do *not* mean good performances. They mean that somebody did not do his work when, or as well, as he should.

Solution of production leadership comes most often with the employment of the professional director. If he is properly trained, a good teacher and organizer, he can usually set up the technical side of the theatre with volunteers so that it will function smoothly with his direction program. Naturally the professional director works constantly toward the day when the organization can hire its second staff member, the designer-technical director.

The "front of the house," second half of the leadership problem, involves all the departments of a theatre other than those concerned with the actual production of the play. In community theatre this is the field of endeavor for the board of directors and committees appointed by them. Here are evolved means for securing audiences and then seeing to their service and comfort by providing a box-office for reservations, furnishing suitable programs, staffing the house with ushers and house managers, and, when coffee is served, providing hosts and hostesses.

In addition to these manifold duties, the board has the larger problems of hiring the director and other employees, approving play selections, and deciding on over-all policies. These are heavy responsibilities and demand, first of all, a civic-minded attitude. It is imperative that board members think constantly of their theatre as part of the civic structure.

I favor complete separation of the board and the production side of theatre. Once the board has hired—or in the case of the volunteer, appointed—the director, it is then his responsibility to produce the play. To do this he must have freedom of authority and he must have confidence which comes from knowing that all the other playhouse departments are functioning properly under the supervision of the board and the committees.

This theory of separate areas of authority implies that persons should not be elected to the board simply because they are good actors or good technicians. Those who are too close to the actual production of the plays usually lack perspective for effective board service. Actors are subject to most human weaknesses, and it is but natural that good players on a board will tend to approve plays in which they see opportunities for themselves. Their position as employers of the director, or his appointers, puts unfair pressure on castings. Far more important is that actual participants in production nearly always are too close to the work for long-range policy thinking.

In towns of limited population, operations may be so small that there are not enough people to man the divided authority plan, but even they will gain if they work toward the idea. In an organization where board members are heads of costumes, properties, lighting, scene construction, and so forth, the full potential of the project has not been realized. If these people are expert technicians, they should be giving all the time and energy they have to technical problems and let their board places be filled by others, perhaps of less theatre talent, who think in terms of making their town a better place to live, and their theatre's opportunity to aid in reaching that objective.

It is wrong to "reward" a good player or technician by election to the board. What that person deserves is further opportunity to use his talent in acting or crew work, and a progressive, growing theatre will bring it to him.

Natural to the young organization is the question, "How can we get our top civic leaders to serve on our board when they feel we have not yet proved ourselves, that we are not yet a civic asset?"

The answer is time, and fidelity to the plan. Also the courage and the wisdom on the part of the first board members, who are usually most interested in play production, to relinquish their board places as soon as the civic leaders will accept them.

Where are the civic leaders? They are all about, and their names are found on the boards of the United Fund, the Red Cross, the symphony, the opera association, and all the other projects conceived and operated for the good and betterment of the community. Such citizens are not too numerous in most towns and they are much in demand for board service. However, in many cases they have learned that after a few years of giving their time and energy to one project they are refreshed and do beter work by going on the board of another endeavor.

This philosophy is vital to building the new concept of community theatre as much more than an organization which simply does plays. It involves the vision of the playhouse as an important factor in the over-all leisuretime program of a progressive town. If we accept this higher objective, then we see that it is no more important for a theatre board member to know how to run a switchboard than it is for a member of the library board to be an expert in the Dewey decimal system.

Our sample constitution (see Chapter Two) stated that board members were elected for three-year terms and could serve no more than two consecutive terms. This guarantee of new blood is valuable. As the organization grows and begins to demonstrate its potential values, civic leaders quite removed from actual play production will begin to agree to board service. These will be the men and women who can think and act in such terms as financing a building program, increasing the number of members, enlarging the service to community and region. Talent of this sort is as important to community theatre as a supply of good leading men or attractive ingenues.

Acquiring top civic leaders for board service is tempered with one restriction: they must be workers on a working board. Lending a name, no matter how important, is rarely enough to justify occupying a seat at the board of directors' table. The time to set this principle is when the nominating committee interviews prospective board members. They should be asked quite frankly if they will be willing to work. This will not offend, but will emphasize the point that the organization has serious work to do.

Allocation of board members to specific tasks is generally the province of the president. A little ingenuity on his part may prove revealing as to the various abilities of board members. At times he can widen participation by use of co-chairmen.

The membership chairman is one of the most important appointments, since the work of this committee will pretty well determine the size of the organization. In Shreveport this post has been held with equal success by board and nonboard personnel. The qualities of the leader and organizer come first.

Box-office chairman is also an important position since it is through box-office service that the organization has its most frequent contact with the member. Again leadership and organizing ability are essential. Many of the larger playhouses hire box-office help, but in Shreveport for thirty-five years the volunteer box-office staff has given an extra touch of cordial service which our members appreciate.

Another important post is the program business manager and here various ladies on the board have served admirably. From the early years an effort ought to be made to establish the theatre's playbill as an advertising medium. It is widely known that the *Playbill*'s of the Broadway theatre hold some of the most expensive and effective advertising space to be found. It is based on the premise that the people who receive them are a choice customer list. This is even more true of a community theatre's membership, with the added advantage that unlike most of the Broadway audience, they will be living in the town where the advertiser does business.

Following this principle of a sound advertising medium, it is better to let the program grow slowly than to accept the type of donation "ads" which fill so many programs and which are the bane of the local merchant. By the time a program has grown to eight pages, a rate card should be established which can be changed and increased as printings and readership increases. Our Shreveport *Playbill* sells for $50 for a quarter page, $100 for a half, and $175 for a full page. The back cover is slightly higher, selling for $225. This is based on six printings each season and three thousand copies per printing. The rates quoted are, of course, for the season.

With a twenty-four page book we can afford the best of printing and the expensive cover photo and still show a profit. Proving that an attractive theatre program has high reader value, frequent checks have shown that more than 90 per cent of our *Playbills* are taken out of the auditorium and carried home by our audiences.

The chairman of ushers can build a sense of participation among the teenagers. Ushering gives high school and college girls an attractive part in theatre activity. Some playhouses use various clubs in their usher plan, assigning a certain night to a particular club. We use four girls each night with an usher corps numbering fifty to seventy-five per season. Working closely with the ushers are the house managers, the gentlemen who take tickets and supervise the front of the house during the performance. Again this is a pleasant way to bring businessmen into a feeling of working with the theatre. Our house chairman uses about fifty different men for this work during the season.

A highly important committee, and one which works throughout the year, is the play reading committee. This function should be confined to board members and, in our experience, we have found that it functions best with a chairman and four members. With one-third of the board constantly at the work of reading plays, it makes decisions about programming rather simple. Working closely with the director, this committee has a highly responsible and rather intricate procedure which is discussed in Chapter Nine.

A difficult and never-ending project for the organization is that of public relations. A first step is the firm establishment of this phrase and its resultant attitude as contrasted with the commonly used term "publicity." The first purpose of newspaper men and the news editors of radio and television stations is, as their name implies, the dissemination of news. Somehow the mere visitation of a "publicity chairman" sets up a withdrawal reflex within these gentlemen. When dramatic groups tell me they have difficulties with the communication media, I always ask, "Do you give them news?" The invariable answer comes, "Well, we offer them lots of publicity."

The theatre as subject matter is essentially newsworthy, but too often the preparation, presentation, and style of theatre news are not in proper journalistic form. A new organization might be wise to have conferences with the various news editors and explain their purpose and their plans. If this discussion bears out the philosophy of building a civic asset, a true community structure, most newsmen will be ready to go along. True, they will expect proof of these stated goals within a reasonable period, and they will ask that news of the work come to them in proper form and at the proper times.

A person with newswriting experience can be found in nearly all civic theatres. Finding such a person to serve as public relations chairman is not the same as asking a working newspaperman or woman to do the job. The very connection of the latter with a specific publication sets up handicaps which tend to overbalance the value of knowing that "our chairman works for the paper or the radio station." Ethically, the double obligation to his employer and to his theatre, can have but one logical outcome and that is to favor the employer. A news medium can, and usually will, do more for an organization if none of its staff holds official position therein.

Assuming the person with news experience to be found, the second step is to lay out a story plan for the over-all season and then a detailed form for the treatment of each play. In the first category will come stories about membership, elections, additions to plant or equipment, and all activities away from play production.

Following the same newsworthy angle, the sequence of production from announcement of the play selected, tryouts, the cast, history of the play, news of the setting, features on unusual backgrounds of players or interesting properties, the box-office opening, and opening night, would indicate eight logical news stories for each play. If these are submitted in proper form and at suggested deadlines, most of them will show up in print. Consideration ought to be given to the usual journalistic premise that the Sunday or other large edition has more room for such items than the daily. It is well also to thank someone for a story which gets a good position and an effective headline and not confine remarks to the papers to complaints about the stories which got "lost."

A shorter story plan will serve for radio and television. Their time is limited for news, but they can be of important help in telling the theatre story. Most television stations have a local interview program and players in the forthcoming production make logical guests.

A solution we evolved in Shreveport seems almost an ideal answer for the problems of this department. A leading public relations firm handles the work of the Shreveport Little Theatre, without charge, as a public service. The professional, efficient handling of our news is obviously of great satisfaction. In the larger towns it will be found that one public relations firm does the Red Cross work as a public service, another the community chest or the symphony. One may readily be found to do a similar job for the community theatre.

One of the basic tenets of community theatre, often learned too late or not at all, is that growth and progress depend heavily on the number of citizens informed and therefore interested in the organization. This is quite different from counting members or participants; this is pure public relations in the broadest sense.

Thus while using the communication media intelligently and with a designed program, we need to do more to make certain that the full meaning of community theatre gets attention from a reasonable, and increasing, proportion of the population.

This is where the human element can be of inestimable value. After all, we are working and talking and selling *live* theatre and those who have not seen the plays have no reason to attach any meaning or importance to the living factor. In the press, no community theatre can compete with the regularity, or the garishness, of the daily movie ads. But if we can expose the citizen to the impact of living theatre, or at least the living person talking of theatre, we may begin to get our message across.

The devices are many. The simplest is the series of talks

before the town's clubs. This is not so easy as it looks: Both speaker and material must be carefully prepared for these appearances. The same speech will hardly be suited for the Garden Clubs if it was exactly right for Rotary, Kiwanis, and Lions. And there are some professional directors who are not adept at public speaking and would find it the better part of wisdom to cast others for such assignments. Above all, any speech for living theatre should be exciting, well delivered, and tend to leave the hearer with a desire to participate.

A more effective instrument than a speech about theatre is a bit of theatre itself. Many organizations have successfully toured short plays in their cities to the ultimate good of their work. But it is not always simple to find suitable scripts, nor do the players often get an even break in the facilities for the performances. Not too many other professions would care to exhibit their work on the bare stage of the civic club; yet actors often dare it.

Obviously, the best impression a theatre can make is when the citizen comes within its walls for productions prepared in the regular manner. We have used several approaches which seem to have merit. Upon occasion we invite the speech and drama students from one of the high schools to be our guests at an early dress rehearsal. These young people make good test audiences for most plays, and in many cases soon appear as regular members and workers.

A commonly used device for widening the base of community interest is the sponsored performance. This gives the purchasing organization opportunity to make a profit by re-selling the tickets, and it brings to the Playhouse that valuable commodity: a new audience. If the names and addresses of these audiences can be secured they make excellent potential sources for future members.

It is possible to interest an entire community in a dramatic enterprise, and when it happens the results are a matter for admiration. Thus far this Utopian situation has occurred chiefly in the rather specialized field of the outdoor dramas of the Southeast. Outstanding examples are the eight dramas written by Paul Green and Kermit Hunter: *The Lost Colony* at Roanoke Island; *The Common Glory*, at Williamsburg; *Unto These Hills* at Cherokee, North Carolina; *The Founders* at Williamsburg; *Wilderness Road* at Berea, Kentucky; *Horn in The West* at Boones, North Carolina; *Chucky Jack* at Gatlinburg, Tennessee and *Thy Kingdom Come* at Roanoke, Virginia. Here are productions involving the entire community and attracting regional and even national attention. Enjoying somewhat the same broad backing of the citizenry are the Shakespearean Festivals at the two Stratfords, Ontario and Connecticut, and those at Yellow Springs, San Diego, and Ashland. A bit further from the straight course of community theatre, but holding the same firm backing of their cities, are the various music theatres at Dallas, St. Louis, Kansas City, and other centers.

In each of these endeavors the impact upon the town or city has been complete, both in wide attention and in economic returns. Of course, some credit goes to the scale of these enterprises. Individual audiences number in the thousands, and often hundreds are working in the production. Yet it is not all a matter of size. These are examples of theatre public relations functioning effectively, consistently, and completely. The residents of the community have been exposed to the idea of the event so continuously that the efforts and energy they have expended seem a small price to pay for the greatness of the achievement.

CHAPTER SEVEN

Where Do Citizens Do Plays in the Community?

"If we only had a home!"

How often have I heard this from theatre groups in the last quarter century. Too many times it has been said with a good deal of emotional content and the overlying implication that a building would, somehow, solve all problems. In 1929, when my wife and I began direction of our first theatre, we used to say it. In Sioux City we found a vigorous organization with a temporary solution of the housing problem. The city had given the Sioux City Little Theatre the top floor of the City Hall for its use.

Here we had an office, two rooms suitable for class work, a large rehearsal room, and a second large area for a scene shop. It was not elaborate, but with a little work it gained some attractiveness. Casting, rehearsals, and scene construction went along well, and it was not until we reached production dates that we realized the difficulties. For one dress rehearsal we would move our players to one of the high schools and suddenly meet our setting and its accouterments. The latter had been dropped, by block and tackle, down the five stories of the City Hall's stairwell!

By the spring of 1930 a downtown house recently vacated by a stock company became feasible; so our moving distance was shortened though it was no less strenuous. At this point we found a vacated church which soon became our projected "home." After a deal of work and remodeling, we were able to open there in the Fall of 1930. A home had been found but it did not remove all problems. A theatre plant, no matter how humble, involves insurance of various kinds, housekeeping, repairs, heating and cooling, and many other expenses invisible in a rented auditorium. It does bring important gains: a new cohesion to the group, the added efficiency of rehearsing and playing on the same stage, and a look of permanence in the town.

The desire and need is natural for the community theatre group but the moves belong in proper sequence. It would be foolhardy for a new organization to build a plant in its first two or three years of operation. At this point, organizational crystallization is still taking place and, even if money is no object, it is doubtful if the right size or kind of theatre can be erected until the organization has more fully defined itself.

There is no chicken-or-the-egg question in the sequence of community theatre progression. A plant cannot bring a vital theatre group into existence, but the group can solve the housing problem. In a few cities about the land stand empty monuments to the fallacy of "We'll build a plant and then we'll organize a theatre." It does not happen often, fortunately, for a discarded or unused theatre is a cause for deep regret when one recalls all the splendid organizations which need them.

An example in point occurred in a large city. A lady with a great deal of money, and not too much certainty about community theatre procedure, decided that the way to get a place where she could act was to build a playhouse. The structure was erected, charming indeed, but the lady could never find a way to make an organization grow within it.

Temporary housing, difficult though it may be, *does* belong in the development of community theatre. The pillar-to-post pattern will test the stamina of the group and, if it survives, give important toughening to the collective spirit. Had we followed the most elementary principles of theatre design in the vast building program of public school auditoria during the last thirty years, community groups would have less frantic times during their temporary housing period.

Most architects are talented and creative artists, but many of them have a curious blind spot in their attitude toward the theatre needs of auditoria. Granted that the principal uses of a high school auditorium are not for the production of drama, still plays have been done by high schools for many years and they will logically occur in the auditorium's schedule. Why then should these astute gentlemen of the drawing board, in chossing between elements of design and materials, nearly always select the ones which will make play production difficult?

A hardwood floor is attractive in many locations but one of them is not on the stage. The glee club can sing as well on pine flooring; the speakers can orate as well standing upon it; but when the poor dramatics teacher is asked to do her play on a hardwood floor, she faces an additional and unnecessary hardship when she is told she may not put stage screws in the polished surface.

This is a simple, but typical, example of the problem. The same architect would not presume to draw up a service station without finding out what provisions the owner wanted made for a greaserack or carwashing. These are not the chief functions of a service station—those occur in the pump area—but they *do* happen and they need the proper structural facilities.

So long as plays are to be done in high school auditoria, the structural and equipping procedures essential to play production ought to be followed, so long as they do not disturb the other uses of the structure. These need not involve additional expense. In fact, many of the crimes against theatre found in auditorium construction have cost *more* than the ways which would have aided theatrical activities.

Taking but one example, the obsolete footlights, the immovable border lights (often in red, white, and blue!) and two or three housebeams focused irrevocably on the orchestra pit cost more than would suitable, flexible, and modern lighting units. School boards apparently like the simple package-deal of the Victorian lighting set-up which they buy so often for the new auditorium, but they should be the first to admit that it is *their* fault when the high school play looks as if it were lighted by an expert left over from the St. Louis Fair.

Whenever theatre people can give advice on construction and equipment problems of a new stage, they are happy to do so. This help is usually given free by directors and designers because they feel that if a new stage can be built properly it may somehow help the total state of theatre. Together they occasionally exert an important force in the cause of better housing. When the American Educational Theatre Association convened at the Los Angeles Statler in Christmas week, 1955, for its annual convention, we heard with alarm that public school authorities of Southern California had decided to eliminate auditoria from new school buildings. This was a new catastrophe. The ill-built affairs with poor sightlines, too many seats, obsolete lighting, hardwood floors, inadequate width and depth and height were bad enough—but no auditorium at all was worse.

The authorities had an answer for our question, "Where will the dramatic arts program take place?" and the answer was a piquant word: cafetorium. But too many directors had suffered with a monstrosity called the gymnatorium to feel enthusiasm for this newest architectural vision. It was quite clear that when the cafetorium had finished serving the meals and the dishes were pushed back the remaining facilities would be hardly ideal for play production.

AETA promptly appointed the wise and capable Horace Robinson of Oregon University to meet with the Los Angeles County school authorities. Through the efforts of Professor Robinson and others, the blight of the cafetorium seems to have been stopped in that section.

Current building costs are forcing school boards to think of all-purpose rooms in new construction, but the program in dramatic arts is too sound, too valuable, and too well established to be handicapped by even worse housing than it has been given in the past.

There is a brighter side to current thinking in high school construction. The Cedar Rapids case will serve as an example. In that Iowa city two new high schools are being built with auditoria scaled to seat *one-half* of the student body. At once this is a gain for theatre. Rather than the vast impossibility of 1500 seats, too large for secondary school play production, the 750-seat auditorium will be far more suitable, not only for the high school program but for any number of community programs which need a medium-sized auditorium. When the rare occasions arise demanding the presence of the entire student body, such sessions can be held in the gymnasium. The two Cedar Rapids schools also plan little theatres, seating less than 300, adjacent to the larger auditorium but with a joint plan of stage construction which will give splendid space and facilities to both auditoria.

Should this progressive thinking spread widely, the community theatres being organized in the years ahead might begin to have quite ideal temporary housing in the high school little theatres, certainly more than adequate until they build their own plants.

Until those happier days arrive, theatre groups will have to use the most suitable auditorium they can find, choosing when possible those with less than 500 seats. Even the finest stars of Broadway in a Pulitzer-Prize play can get "lost" in an auditorium which is too large. The small seating capacity also has the virtue of requiring repeated performances, an essential to the growth of players and community theatres.

There are towns in which no suitable auditorium is to be had and, for a group in such a situation, it would seem best to turn to arena staging. This brings the housing problem down to the bare essentials of four walls and a roof. In the case of the late and lamented Margo Jones, it was shown that an acting company could have a long and exciting career in nothing more eaborate than an exhibit building at the State Fair Grounds in Dallas. Hotel ballrooms have often been used for arena groups and there are a few plants deliberately constructed as arenas.

As Donald Oenslager said at a convention of the Southwest Theatre Conference, "The arena theatre is an economic expedient." With the cost of scenery removed, production-in-the-round offers an attractive solution for the group with limited finances. In the last few years there has been a rediscovery of the arena idea, although it was as long ago as 1932 that Glenn Hughes did his first production in Mr. and Mrs. Murphy's penthouse atop the Edmond Meany Hotel in Seattle. Three years later, Professor Hughes opened his new Penthouse Theatre on the University of Washington campus.

I do not see the arena stage as the form of the future, any more than I think we are irrevocably bound to the standard proscenium. Suitability of plays for in-the-round production and maintenance of aesthetic distance are two of the difficulties. The most ardent arena fans who say, "We can do anything," will, in the production of such a play as *Mr. Roberts,* back up against one wall of their room and improvise a sort of Shakespearian apron stage. I do not quarrel with the solution, but I do not consider it producing *Mr. Roberts* in the round.

This problem of play selection can be solved by the judicious; but the failure of the audience to find, or keep, aesthetic distance from the play is a more serious obstacle to successful arena production. It is not so much that the acting is sometimes in your lap, or that one-fourth of the time you must be content with a display of derrières, but that there is no way to separate players and audience in the spectator's line of vision. Unknowingly, theatre audiences appreciate the center-of-attention principle, as the director has used it on the stage, but the members of that audience do not apply it to themselves. Thus the most capable players wage a losing fight against the crossing and uncrossing legs and wiggling arms and heads of the audience behind them but in the remaining spectators' line of vision. I defy the most intent playgoer to stay in the scene when one of those extroverts, who seem to feel they are "right in the show" when seated at an arena's front row begins to "react."

Albert McCleery, the distinguished television producer, and creator of the "Cameo" technique, tried to solve this problem of the divided center of attention when he headed the theatre at Fordham University. He dropped a scrim around the arena stage which did shut off the audience on the far side but tended to give an "enchanted" air to every production, and gave the players some nice problems for entrances and exits.

Until the community theatre is ready to build its new plant in the obvious range of the flexible stage, it is better to remodel along proscenium lines. There are many examples of organizations which have looked at existing buildings with imagination, and their resulting playhouses, while perhaps not ideal, have made possible sound and continuing production programs. A few of these may serve as examples of what can be done, and perhaps persuade present and future community theatre groups to take another look and find solutions for housing in buildings which now stand in their towns.

The Memphis Little Theatre needed a home badly. When Clarence Saunders' Pink Palace became municipal property, someone in the theatre looked again and again at the mansion's empty swimming pool. The only possible connection with the structure of a theatre was the gently sloping concrete floor. That was enough. Taking out the wall at one end, a stage was constructed, seats installed on the swimming pool floor, other alterations made, and the Memphis Little Theatre was in business in its new home. Many years have passed since this "temporary" solution was found, but meantime the Memphis Little Theatre has had a fine career.

In 1888 a little Mormon Church was built at Williams Bay, Wisconsin, near the lovely shores of Lake Geneva. By 1930 the building was no longer needed as a church, and in 1934 the two-year-old Lake Geneva Drama Club moved into it for production of their plays. Purchasing the building in 1938, the group now known as the Belfry Players added a large stage-house and have enjoyed an excellent production record.

Much older than the church at Lake Geneva was the building first used as the Governor's Mansion in New Orleans before the Louisiana Purchase, situated on Jackson Square and facing the St. Peter Street side of the Cabildo. In 1916 the Drawing Room Players began to do plays in one of the Pontalba Apartments, also on Jackson Square. When the organization became Le Petit Théâtre du Vieux Carré in 1919, the old Governor's Mansion seemed a likely prospect for the new theatre. Without destroying the historic charm of the site, the theatre was built and has served through the decades as one of America's most important community playhouses.

The Rochester (New York) Community Players recently

took a good look around their city and found a Howard Johnson Restaurant building for sale. By a clever use of the structure as the auditorium, they were able to contrive a theatre plan of considerable space and effectiveness.

Another solution by a Wisconsin group is the picturesque one evolved by the Haylofter's Inc. of Burlington, founded in 1932. The members met at the old Newell barn where they presented one-acts and evolved their name. For eleven years they sought a home and at last solved their problem by buying the Muth Malt House for back taxes due Racine County. Exuding drama, the Malt House stands like a medieval castle along the banks of the Fox River. It was built in 1872 with the lime used in the mortar prepared on the premises and the fieldstone hauled to the site by teams of oxen.

Today the Haylofters have an outer and inner foyer and an auditorium seating 125. The project has been a long and difficult one but the resulting setting has a unique charm and quality, and a real sense of belonging to the Wisconsin soil and landscape.

A more common path to theatre facilities is through the surburban movie house. Hundreds of these small structures have been shuttered in recent years as Hollywood has been forced to the fewer-pictures-and-better-ones and the keep-open-the-houses-that-pay policy. They offer a number of advantages to the community theatre in that the structure itself, built as a theatre, has many usable features. There is a lobby, often small, an auditorium with a sloping floor, and quite frequently adequate heating and cooling equipment.

There is seldom more than a platform for the screen, but in most cases the auditorium is a bit too long and extension of the stage into it works well. Two of the organizations which have solved their housing in this manner are the Des Moines Community Playhouse and the Footlighters Community Theatre of Cedar Rapids. In both cases the buildings contain a cubic footage far larger than they could have built new at current prices. By extending stage areas and installing proper equipment, both organizations have attractive and valuable plants. The Des Moines Playhouse has such a splendid basement area that part of it serves for rehearsals and class work of the Children's Theatre.

These are but a few of the theatres that have found homes by remodeling. Almost any town or city has an existing building or buildings which, treated imaginatively, can be transformed into a workable playhouse. From a cost approach, it is the cheapest way to acquire space and cubic footage.

By implication, the expensive way to housing is through new construction, and yet it is the way to exact realization of needs. A first step is to examine the record of the organization, its rate of growth, its importance in the civic pattern, and the relation of its present housing to the service rendered by the organization.

If these answers indicate a real need for new construction, then careful estimates are needed as to the amount of money which might be raised. This will vary with the economic patterns of the various towns or cities. Advice from economic and financial experts outside the organization should be sought, since their opinions will not be colored by undue enthusiasm for theatre itself.

When the Omaha Community Playhouse decided that it had to do something about a new plant, answers were sought and found to such questions. Built in 1928, the first Playhouse was put up strictly as a temporary structure, with none of the builders aware that it would be used for twenty-eight years. As Omaha citizens set to work on the problem, they found a correlation between adequate housing and theatre attendance. Taking the season of 1948-49 as a point of comparison, it was

learned that the Denver Civic Theatre, operating in it magnificent new structure, had by 1956 enjoyed an increase of 95.7
per cent in attendance, although the population of Denver had
increased but 28 per cent in the same period.

The Des Moines Community Playhouse, in its remodeed
building, had an increase of 47.6 per cent in attendance while
the city gained but 15.4 per cent. The people of Omaha then
counted again and found that their old plant had seen but a
6.8 per cent attendance increase although the city had grown
by 30 per cent.

After careful examination of these and other figures and
facts, the people of the Omaha Playhouse moved ahead and set
up an active campaign for a $300,000 plant. Their attractive
brochure indicated a breadth of support and a soundness of
thinking which has led to success. Listed were breakdowns in
building and equipment items so that donors might select
items suited to their means. A few of them point up the fact
that new construction and equipment are far from inexpensive. Auditorium seats, of which there are twenty-one rows,
will cost $900 per row. The air-conditioning system is listed
at $30,000, while the rehearsal and social room may be
financed for $9000. The upper lobby will cost $36,000 and
the lower lobby $30,000. $90,000 will pay for the auditorium,
while the lighting equipment is set at $24,000 and the rigging
and curtains are to cost $60,000.

There are many more items but the point is made that
building a new theatre is not a matter to be approached lightly.
That we have so many excellent plants about the land is proof
that towns and cities have backed their belief in the value of
their theatres by money in large amounts.

Financing a building program is a variable procedure rang-
ing from the single donor, who pays the entire cost, to the
usual fundraising drive which appeals to the entire city. Be-

tween those extremes are the plans such as the large gift by an individual which is to be matched by fundraising. The Omaha plan is an example of the memorial gift idea, in which the various sections of the Playhouse will be marked by plaques bearing the name of the donor, or the person or family memorialized. The Omaha Playhouse also suggests that pledges be paid over a period of three years, since donors may take advantage of a tax deduction for three consecutive years.

Two of the cities enjoying playhouses built by one individual are Kalamazoo and Denver. Dr. Upjohn, Kalamazoo civic leader, gave his city the fine Civic Auditorium which the Civic Players use in conjunction with other organizations. Housed for years on the campus of the University of Denver, the Denver Civic Theatre not long ago received a new home through the generosity of Miss Helen Bonfils, who has given the Theatre and Denver one of the most impressive plants in America. The Bonfils Memorial Theatre was constructed at a cost of $1,210,-000. It was financed entirely by the F. G. Bonfils Foundation created by Miss Bonfils' father and which she serves as president. In writing me about this magnificent project, Miss Bonfils said, "I can think of no better way to help people with enjoyment and culture than a fine Playhouse with complete facilities and an adequate working staff."

Whatever plan is followed in paying for new construction, it is highly important that the approach be sound at all times and that the organization do not overreach itself. In planning, great care should be taken to include all essential equipment since this looms large in theatre building budgets.

A major building program by a community theatre has to be faced as a financial problem outside normal operating expenses. Occasionally an organization sets aside part of each season's income for a building fund. This seems contrary to the announced spirit of the usual incorporation "as a nonprofit, educational institution," and it leads one to suspect that the money could be well spent on some phase of operation. The extremely low cost-per-play of the community theatre membership makes saving any of that income difficult except, of course, for those organizations which do not employ a director; and in those situations the small surpluses would be better set aside for the purpose of securing a full-time professional to head the organization. To hope to earn any substantial part of the cost of a new theatre plant out of operating income does not seem logical, probable, or feasible.

With the decision to build, and a sound financing scheme under way, the organization has to decide on the kind of plant it wants. Despite all the clamor for doing away with the proscenium stage and for building ony in the realm of space, apron, and the other variations, most of the important new plants have remained safely within conventional boundaries. I do not know that this is the *right* road, only that it is the most *traveled*. When the time arrives to spend $200,000 to $1 million on a playhouse, a certain caution creeps in, coming perhaps from the joint backgrounds of architects and building committees. The tendency is to build theatres which resemble existing theatres.

Exceptions to this general trend include Fred Koch Jr.'s Ring Theatre at the University of Miami. It has incorporated the best features of proscenium and arena staging with a flexible seating arrangement based on movable ramps. This interesting experiment did not occur, however, when a *community* organization faced building but happened in the rarified and glamorous atmosphere of Florida and at one of its *universities*. The Euclid-77th Street Theatre in Cleveland, which follows the general plan and style of the Greco-Roman and Elizabethan stages with apron extending into the auditorium, was again not a typical community situation; for it is the third auditorium of the Cleveland Play House which, along with the Pasadena Playhouse, has developed in a private and special area midway between the true community theatre and showbusiness.

For real daring in theatre design in recent years, we have to turn to several of the new plants in Europe. There is hope for an exciting new treatment of theatre construction as Frank Lloyd Wright's Dallas Theatre Center nears reality. Yet even America's master-artist of modern design has not completely eliminated the proscenium principle.

While we wait for the dreamers to design and *prove* the superiority of a new form of theatre building, let us examine the way a community group can move toward construction of a plant which is functional, efficient, comfortable, and not extravagant. All of us understand that a playhouse is divided into two parts: the audience area and the performance area. Would that all of us also understood that unless the latter is properly built and adequately equipped there may be difficulty in finding enough people who want to use the former.

At this bare starting point we can usually detect inadequacies in the architect. In too many cases this talented expert designs lobbies, box-offices, restrooms, and auditoria quickly, happily—and expensively. Whenever a community theatre building committee finds their architect devoting most of his time and conversation to the front of the house, it is time to beware. The objective, the reason for all the effort, is the heart of a theatre plant, the stage area. Unless there is understanding of this essential truth and at least a willingness to listen and take advice, the final result is apt to be another inadequate or crippled theatre.

It might be worth while if every architect retained to build a community theatre could make a pilgrimage to Fayetteville, Arkansas. There, amid the Ozarks, on the campus of Arkansas

University stands a magnificent example of a theatre built with the highest fidelity to purpose. The stagehouse is one of the finest and best equipped in America, it consumed the major portion of the money, and before it are but 300 seats in a simple, pleasant auditorium. It is small wonder that Virgil Baker, Blair Hart, and the other staff members work so happily in such a setting. They have a fine and proper instrument for their purpose. The size of their stage is indicated by the fact that they can set up a complete arena theatre on it.

I hold that a community theatre should not be built with more than 500 seats with perhaps 400 ideal. This makes for high quality seating and allows the playhouse to practice that vital training procedure of repeated performances.

Surprising to some is the fact that comfort and good sightlines do not add cost to auditorium construction, but they are factors which have to be put in at the beginning; it is hard to go back and correct an inadequate slope in the floor of the house. That slope should be at least one inch for each foot, although some plants, like the University of Iowa Theatre, have successfully used a far steeper pitch.

The arrangement of the seats themselves is an inexpensive way to audience comfort and satisfaction. A personal preference is for the continental seating plan, which allows forty-five inches from seatback to seatback. This eliminates aisles, except at the side of the auditorium, since there is easy access and egress past occupied seats. There are cities whose fire laws prohibit continental seating, and those localities will have to settle for the three-bank plan: a minimum of thirty-four inches seatback to seatback and aisles at least forty inches wide on either side of the center section and at either side of the auditorium. This has obvious advantages over the two-bank plan whose center aisle takes out the best seats in the house.

It is wise to hold the width of the front row of seats to

that of the proscenium arch and to fan out the width of rows never past valid sightlines. Staggering the seats greatly adds to the value of each individual sightline.

A foyer large enough to duplicate the playing area of the stage has been found by some playhouses to have added value as a rehearsal room. It and the other elements about it—rest-rooms, offices, and box-office—ought to be conservatively designed and economically treated.

An element which demands care, and some money, is the acoustical treatment of the auditorium. Here is where a specialist, an acoustical engineer, may well be worth his fee. The shape and volume of the auditorium will determine the amount and position of sound-absorbing material necessary to control reverberation. Avoiding concave surfaces will tend to eliminate echo.

Good seeing and hearing conditions, guided by frugality, ought to make the new audience area suitable and efficient at a minimum cost.

As we cross the curtain line we come to the laboratory where living theatre is to be created; the magic space where characters and their habitats appear to entertain, edify, and inspire; the *raison d'être* of theatre. Here the larger part of our money is to be spent and spent well.

I have never talked to a director who said his stage was large enough, but certainly we should try to give him all possible living room for his creations. A proscenium opening of thirty to thirty-four feet seems sufficient and is a commonly found specification. It is the space behind the proscenium that can help or hinder play production. The depth should at least equal the proscenium opening, and a dimension of one and a half times the opening is far better.

A simple and usually adequate yardstick for stage width is to build it three times as wide as the proscenium. If we apply these ideas to a thirty-foot proscenium we give the director a stage forty-five feet deep and ninety feet wide. This should give adequate space for most productions and does not become too formidable in cost until we start to take the stagehouse skyward. Here construction costs mount frighteningly and have made a number of new plants forget the old rule-of-thumb which said that a stagehouse ought to be two and a half times the height of the proscenium. The height of the arch can vary from fifteen to twenty feet with seventeen seeming adequate for a 400-seat house. This woud mean that the hypothetical stagehouse with grid and working space above should rise to fifty feet.

Many new plants have gridirons soaring far higher, and yet in the modern practice of stagecraft this represents in many cases a waste of money in these great, and often partly-used, boxes. The wagon stages, revolving stages, and other current shifting devices call less and less for the old-fashioned flying of scenery. A sound way to cut the cost of a stagehouse is to limit the grid to twice the height of the proscenium arch.

Any architect who has built an auditorium can quickly specify a counterweight system of twenty-five sets of lines, and another large figure goes into the construction budget. But today we do not need such elaborate flying facilities in modern stage practice, and it would seem discreet to install a few obviously needed sets and complete the counterweight system at a later date when it proves to be needed.

A simple step at this point, but one with great future value, is to decide to use the back wall of the stagehouse as a cyclorama. This requires that it be kept free of fittings or projections and that it be treated in a sand-float plaster. Of course it will not serve when sky effects are called for downstage to right or left of a setting. This occasional contingency led a few theatres about the land to the appalling solution of building plaster sky-domes around their playing areas. Now these monstrosities sit with throttling and immovable grandeur defying directors to do anything about them.

The shaped canvas cyclorama hung on a curved batten is in common usage and seems to come closest to serving designers' demands for sky. It contains a second curved batten at the bottom with the downstage sections removable when necessary for shifting. Again this piece of equipment is not immediately necessary, and could be deferred in favor of a few more lighting units.

The monies wasted in school auditoria for so-called "lighting equipment" are often matched by unwary building committees in the community theatre. It should be made common knowledge that the spotlight is the best device for lighting a stage and that an instrument to control its volume, a switchboard, is also required. From this alpha beginning we can proceed honestly to install the proper number of lighting units in the proper locations.

The best lighting for an individual actor at a given moment on a stage comes from two spotlights which are forty-five degrees above horizontal, halfway between straight up and straight ahead, and forty-five degrees on the horizontal, halfway between straight ahead and straight to one side. The two units are ninety degrees apart with respect to the actor and the horizontal.

Applying this principle to installation, the apron area of our stage and a space six feet behind the curtain call for units mounted in the auditorium. These are known as beam lights or housebeams, and their location becomes a matter of concern when the auditorium is being designed. Occasionally an actual beam is used for their installation, although it is best to maintain access to each lamp from the attic area. The instruments for beam lighting are ellipsoidals, and two should be installed for eight feet of proscenium width. Their size is determined by their throw, the distance the light travels to the actor. The 500-watt ellipsoidal with a six-inch lens can handle a thirty-foot throw while the 750-watt lamp is effective to fifty feet, a distance which may be necessary if the auditorium ceiling is high.

The first pipe batten behind the teaser takes up the task of lighting the acting areas above the six-foot space covered by the house beams. The same forty-five degree principle is used and the 400- or 500-watt fresnels are the proper instruments for the work. Twelve to fifteen of these with six-inch lenses will do an adequate job for most productions when used in conjunction with the eight housebeams.

There is little use for border lights except in conjunction with cyclorama work when they will be needed at both top and bottom, with one six-foot section for each ten linear feet of cyclorama. If the back wall of the stagehouse is to serve as a permanent cyc, the bottom border lights can be installed to fold into the floor when not in use.

Footlights have some possible use in lighting the curtain before the play begins; otherwise none. I have always been grateful that Clarence King, when he designed the Shreveport Little Theatre in 1926, specified, "No footlights!"

Care should be taken to install a sufficient number of stage outlets, at least eight to ten on each side of the stage.

If this basic equipment is so installed as to be completely flexible and access is provided easily to each instrument, then we need only connect our units to an adequate switchboard. This, alas, is easier said than done.

The electronic boards are obviously the best, and yet for a community group financing a new building they seem fantastically expensive. Good lighting can be managed with less elaborate devices such as the auto-transformer. A number of manufacturers turn out good ones, and it seems wise today to decide on the capacity of the board and have it made to specifications rather than paying about as much for a so-called "standard" board. A half dozen 1000-watt dimmers, and six of 2000-watt capacity, placing each set in series with a master dimmer, will take care of all usual dimming requirements.

The location of the switchboard is important; it should be in front of the curtain, preferably in the balcony. It is possible to work from the beam position, but the operator's view of the stage is less distorted from a balcony or projection-booth angle.

There has been some to-do recently about Linnebach projectors. This is not a new instrument though it may be unfamiliar to people who never played with magic-lantern slides as children. It is not, at any rate, an essential piece of equipment.

Careful selection of the architect and the services of a theatre consultant such as Professor Edward C. Cole of Yale University will do much to eliminate building mistakes before they happen.

Flexibility, efficiency, comfort, and beauty—these are the four points from which the imagination should soar, as we visualize and plan our future theatres. However, the playhouse will still be a place for creating and enjoying the play, and it could be that the written form somehow determines the limits of architectural variance. It may be well to ponder the fact that after three-and-a-half centuries the best place and the best way to do Shakespeare's plays is on reproductions of the stage which existed when he wrote them. The stages in use when Ibsen, Chekhov, O'Neill, Shaw, Sherwood, Anderson, and Miller did their work could exert a restraining influence on flights of architectural fancy even three centuries hence.

Sample Theatre Building Budgets

I.

AMARILLO LITTLE THEATRE

Amarillo, Texas   Oma Link Rowley, director

The story of the building of the Amarillo Little Theatre which opened during the 1955-56 season is typical of the long-range efforts which have culminated in the construction of so many fine community theatre plants across the country.

According to Mrs. Nita Krupp, president of the Amarillo Theatre, dreams of the new building go almost back to the opening night of the theatre, December 12, 1927. The first definite step toward realization came with the acquisition of a valuable piece of property. On this was placed a surplus war building, which was used for a workshop for rehearsals and scene shop. During this period performances were given in the rented City Auditorium.

The original property was then sold and the new site purchased. It has increased in value due to the construction of a shopping center of which the theatre is a part. It also gives greatly increased parking areas. The lot is 200 by 300 feet. On this a workshop was built with an area of 2400 square feet. This included the stage, workshop, dressing rooms with showers and toilets. The structure is brick and the proscenium was closed in with lumber to be removed when the second half of the plant was erected. This first section cost $50,000.

Wisely, the organization paid off this amount and accumulated $20,000 before starting the auditorium half of the plant. This construction cost $120,000, which meant that the Amarillo Theatre assumed a mortgage of $100,000 to be met with monthly payments on a fifteen-year loan through a local insurance company, the Western National. The theatre now has 15,000 square feet of space, not including a covered porch which runs from the front entrance along the building to a port cochere.

CONSTRUCTION COSTS

Stage half of plant	$ 50,000
Auditorium half	120,000
Lighting equipment	7,000
Air-conditioning vents and blower	11,000
(Air-conditioning equipment will be added later)	
Plumbing in the front of the house	7,000
Paving	3,000
Total	$198,000

II.

MIDLAND COMMUNITY THEATRE PROJECT

Midland, Texas   Art Cole, director

The site is in West Midland, approximately 260 by 220 feet.

At the rear of the property stands a 25- by 50-foot masonry building now serving as a scene shop.

With streets on three sides of the property, there will be parking for some three hundred cars.

The above assets have existed for six years while the Midland organization has worked to plan and engineer the financing and construction of the new plant. Two separate schemes were brought to blueprint stage but cost estimates kept them from realization. Now a budget in the neighborhood of $125,000 is set up. This is achieved by using a 10,000-square-foot "tent-type" prefabricated metal building shell, common in the Southwestern oil country, but with masonary side walls.

Four hundred and twenty seats, all within forty-five feet of the low out-thrust platform stage, are arranged in a 120-degree circle sweep. The row-platforms graduate in eight-inch increments, and all seats will be directors chairs. No loft will be constructed. Lighting will project from a "flattened 'U'-shaped cloud" platform suspended across the entire auditorium immediately in front of the stage and extending toward the rear for fifteen feet. Facilities for control of lighting, sound, and 16 mm.-motion-picture equipment are at the rear of the auditorium on an upper level.

Dressing-rooms back up the stage and scene-bays flank the stage, which is fifty feet wide. Removable panels, two rows deep, at front center can produce a small orchestra pit. Facilities off the main entrance lobby include concession space, box-office, director's office, rest rooms, janitor's closet, and access to the projection booth.

THE COST ESTIMATES

General construction
Metal building shell	$ 35,000
Other steel and reinforced concrete	15,000
Masonry, plaster, and allied work	15,000
Carpentry, painting, finishing	20,000
Electrical work	10,000
Plumbing	8,000
Heating and air-conditioning	15,000
Special stage lighting	13,500
Seating	2,000
Total	$133,500

Sample Remodeled-Building Project

FOOTLIGHTERS COMMUNITY THEATRE

Cedar Rapids, Iowa   Don Tescher, director

Like many other community theatres, the Footlighters solved a thirty-year search for a permanent home by purchasing the Strand Theatre, a former suburban movie house, and remodeling it into an attractive and efficient theatre plant. As the figures show, they received a great deal for their money and today own a Playhouse which might have cost four times as much had they tried new construction.

Purchase of building and property	$11,576.20
Construction	6,639.12
Plumbing	2,589.58
Wiring for building	2,080.11
Theatre production equipment	1,221.27
Excavation	1,108.25
Heating	1,103.00
Repairs and cleaning	866.85
Decorating and furnishings	770.12
Taxes and administrative	716.40
Wiring for stage and light booth	700.00
Ventilation	544.82
Supplies	82.63
Total	$29,998.35

In addition, materials and labor in the amount of $9,200 was given to the project.

Materials contributed (lumber, hot water heater, gas burner, paint, etc.)	4,800
Labor contributed	2,800
Materials at cost, saving	1,600
Total	$ 9,200
Total dollar value of plant	$39,198.35

CHAPTER EIGHT

The Director

The transitory quality of a theatre performance is a matter for regret in a discussion of the modern director. How quickly I could make my points if I could say, "Here is a performance of *Macbeth* playing in 1850 and, here beside it, is the same play as it is playing one hundred years later. Please notice, if you will, how the advent of the director has made the second production so much easier to watch, to hear, to enjoy. You will observe in the earlier play how the actors ignore such principles as repose, concentration, listening, the center of attention and all the other techniques which a director uses. What's that? You say those 1850 players make you nervous with their rantings, their running about, their wriggling? Very well, let's put the two performances away till we need them again."

Unfortunately living theatre, with all its faults before the day of the modern director, is gone forever. The few photographs, the brief writings about this play or that actor, are all we have left. It was once said that the motion picture would at last provide a permanent way of recording theatre, but alas it does not provide a true record even of its own past performances. As we watch the "late" movies on television, knowing that they are late only in hour and aged in every other respect, we find ourselves thinking, "That picture has changed since I saw it first in 1930."

The film has not changed but we, and the world around

us, have changed. The performances of Chester Morris or Nancy Carroll which entertained us in 1930 are out of key with the modern audience. If the filmed performances of less than thirty years ago seem quaint, how much further removed would be the stage productions of 1890 if we could raise the curtain on them today. In the "good old days" the visiting star would stop by the Opera House late in the afternoon and, addressing the respectful resident company, would say, "In this scene I will be here, and then there, and in this scene I will make my entrance thus. Just remember, stay out of my way!"

Rehearsal? There was little done in the modern sense before 1890. It was considered bad form to "act" before the night of performance. Then, and especially in the case of the visiting star, the rockets would begin to soar and the scenery would be well chewed from footlight to backdrop. It amused Grandfather, for his eyes were chiefly for the virtuoso talents of Bernhardt, Booth, Duse, or Mansfield. The other people in the play? Well, someone had to give the cues so the star could act.

The concept of the artist-director came with the rise of the European Art Theatre that gave the American community theatres their first reason for existence. It was hard for show-business to accept this new authority and there are still old actors and actresses who insist on using, with condescension, the term "stage manager" when speaking of a director. His appearance on the theatre scene was in direct opposition to the old star system. "That man telling me how to play a scene? Ridiculous!"

But this new figure in theatre's over-all dramatis personae, The Man Who Came to Direct, stayed on to become perhaps the dominant factor in the modern theatre. In a century in which the dramatists have not soared with the immortals, the directors have given theatre a procedure, a set of standards, and a level of performance quality hitherto unknown. They have brought new excellence to the Broadway stage and they have made community theatre possible and progressive.

There is a wide variance in the backgrounds, training, and talents of the assemblage of theatre workers we now lump together under the general title "director." It is a matter for regret that this key figure in our theatre is still so new that he has not yet acquired exact definition. We do it better in music, where the person who guides a small group of musicians through their paces is called "the leader." When the formal term "conductor" is used, we imply in our very tone the dignity which that master musician has earned and deserves. A single name cannot accurately include both the distinguished professional directors of the American theatre and those who attempt the work for one or two productions.

Knowing that the full-time professional director is found in only a minority of the community theatres, let us first observe the situation and the possibilities of the volunteer. It is vital to begin with a full awareness of a director's importance in theatre. Once an organization understands that this individual determines more definitely than any other the success or failure of the entire project, then perhaps, the citizens involved in the selection of a volunteer director will begin to see it as a matter of some import.

This discussion is not directed to the ex-professional director who may do one play for his organization without fee; his background and responsibilities should be those of the professional. The concern here is with the man or woman, not academically or professionally trained in the field of direction, who volunteers or is drafted to direct plays for a community theatre.

If this is a sudden decision, with no time for preparation

of a year or so, then we have to make the best of it, but the public should not be led to expect much better results than they would if their favorite college football team was being taught by one of the players. No one would expect even a good *player* immediately to acquire such *coaching* talent that his charges could defeat Oklahoma as coached by Bud Wilkinson.

The number of excellent community organizations which use volunteer directors is evidence that growth and progress in this phase of the work is more than possible. The quality of work done by such organizations as the Players Club of Swarthmore and the Toledo Repertoire Theatre illustrates how far development of the idea can go. At last report not one of the more than seventy member groups of the New Jersey Theatre League had a full-time paid director and yet many of the member organizations do excellent work. But it takes time and study, attributes which are not immediately attainable. A talent for directing is rare and it needs development. Assigning directorial work to a small group of volunteers is a first step and helps eliminate the catastrophes which occur, on the one hand, when the assignments are passed around promiscuously and on the other, when a single inexperienced person is given more than he can handle. A starting point might be to try to find potential directors equal in number to the season's productions.

Once selected, the group, either through self-inspiration or outside encouragement, should begin a course of study. Books on direction are few, and not always satisfactory, but they need to be read. The directing group ought to see as much good theatre as possible, watching it objectively in an effort to learn the practice and application of principles of directing. By hard work and the passage of years, the volunteer directors can become proficient.

Perhaps nowhere else in the theatre group is the building of team spirit more important than with the directors. They need to think constantly of their work as part of a whole, each of their plays being a *part* of a *season*. This will help them to be fair about castings, and avoid the very human tendency to make their own play a personal, highly spotlighted project. Sacrifice of personal glory for the good of the theatre is a price the volunteer director must be willing to pay.

If there is to be progress, a standard of procedures needs establishment, so that the succession of plays has a reasonable and practical rhythm. Tryout patterns, rehearsal schedules for both days and hours, the number of dress rehearsals, and all other time factors are best when uniform, so that players do not have to learn a new timetable for each director.

Finally, the organization owes the volunteer director freedom to work and the dignity commensurate with the position. Full right to cast his own play is an inalienable prerogative so long as he keeps the good of the play first. If he cannot hold this paramount objective in mind at this starting point, he will not likely go far in his avocational directing career. He should also be allowed closed rehearsals, standard practice of the commercial theatre and of professional community theatre directors. Visitors have no more place at rehearsal than they do in the operating room; the time for visiting is when the patient has been returned to his room or, in the case of drama, when the opening night curtain goes up.

The following discussion of the professional director also deeply concerns the volunteer. It may indicate avenues of learning and show the breadth of preparation and the high demands which will come to one who would have a career as a community theatre director.

For some years community theatre people have been imploring the educational theatre to adjust curriculae for more accurate training of directors. Too many drama departments are still turning out an end product for markets which cannot buy. As long ago as October 1941 *The Quarterly Journal of Speech* carried an article of mine entitled, "A Curriculum Plan for a Major in Play Directing." Briefly, it assumed selection of the Direction Major in the Junior year, if personal and talent capabilities justified it. From there on through the M.A., the Direction course would be aimed toward the dual objectives of proficiency in direction and learning basic facts about community theatre management and the director's relation to a community. Public relations and sociology would be important subjects. Following the M.A., the embryo director ought to be ready for his apprenticeship.

So went the long ago article and yet, in many drama departments, it would be news today. In one of the rare attempts to move firmly ahead in curriculum revision, Samuel Selden at the University of North Carolina proposed a new title for completion of work at the doctorate level in areas of drama. His term is Licentiate in Drama rather than Ph.D. Behind the new degree is a realistic preparation which, in the case of the director, involves a full season of directing a community theatre. The business manager spends a year actually running the business affairs of a theatre project and the playwright has to produce playable manuscripts.

This turning away from research in the sixth and seventh years of university theatre training, in favor of active participation in the various areas, is a constructive step, and yet Professor Selden has found little enthusiasm for it among his fellow heads of drama departments. Until we begin to educate the top of the university administrations to the realities and possibilities of the community theatre field, progress at the curriculum level will be slow. Much Ph.D. work will continue to be nothing more than the digging out and reburying of old bones, and university faculties will continue to think along the lines of the frequently uttered statement: "Yes, you're right to finish your degree before you try to act on Broadway. If you don't make it acting, you can still teach. And if you don't like teaching, there's always community theatre!" This would be funny if it were not said so seriously.

My plan of director training after the M.A. involves an essential apprenticeship period at minimum salary. The ideal solution is to have one or two years with an established playhouse as assistant director. Here the theories of community theatre practice are in full operation. All the special techniques aside from direction can be studied and observed. This, plus the opportunity to practice directing, should round out the educational process to the point where the young apprentice may be able to try his own theatre. This has happened in our own organization and in other playhouses; the year or two of intensive practical work in a going theatre seems to make for stability and success when the apprentice goes on his own. The reverse approach is also well known: fine young people finishing at top university drama departments, going directly from campus to a full directing post—and meeting failure.

This is a point at which the enthusiasm of youth needs tempering. The beginning director ought to look for, nay he should seek, an organization befitting his own state of development. This is not easy, for young people have always regarded the oyster of the world as a simple challenge waiting only for their opening.

The reason for not starting above the proper point on the scale is double-edged: trying too large a job will probably result in failure for the director, and the organization may be hurt badly. It is at this stage where community theatre suffers most from the matter of salaries. The small theatres, the beginning organizations, cannot pay much, but the young director ought not to be looking for money. If he is, then the temptation of larger starting stipends, perhaps in teaching, will probably win him away from the field.

What he needs, and what he must want, is the opportunity to direct, to head his own theatre. Counterbalancing those beginners who left community theatre for the riches of television, teaching, or trade are others who so firmly aspired to a career in directing that, finding no position, they founded theatres of their own. Perhaps the hardest way to start, it has resulted in growing theatres where there were none and in the development of a number of youthful directors to the point where they were ready for larger assignments.

If our young apprentice has held fast to the one ambition, an opportunity to direct on his own, and has been hired, then the next great decision involves seeing the job through. If there are no insurmountable problems, the young director ought to plan on staying at the post for five years. A variable figure, of course, yet it will give a long-range character to thinking and planning which will be instrumental in learning and establishing viewpoints.

The transitory attitude among so many community theatre directors has done harm to their own careers and slowed the growth of many organizations. Not long ago a young colleague of mine, in his third theatre post, wanted to leave after two years. He was convinced that the talked-of building would never materialize. At last I convinced him that he should give the position three more years, thinking of it in terms of a five-year project. Dramatically at the end of the five years his organization opened a fine new plant and had it paid for! Now my friend is happily settled for what I trust will be at least a new ten-year project.

Only with the tranquillity of some permanence can the director begin to think of building a community's theatre with the solid foundation and broad structure it needs. Now he can go beyond the restless philosophy characteristic of those who think only of "putting on a play." He and the organization can move up the road which leads to community theatre as an important factor of the civic picture. Short-range ideas and erratic methods will start to disappear as stability grows.

Of course this assumes that the candidate for a directing career is possessed of all the necessary attributes of character to win his proper position in the town. In community theatre it does little good to have it said, "The show was all right but no one can stand the director." This is not showbusiness. The director in community theatre has to be both artist and citizen.

In addition to personal and civic stature, the young director has to prove his excellence as a teacher. The teaching skill required in community theatre needs not only to be highly developed but to be used under the most difficult conditions. Community theatre has no weapons for inducing cooperation, such as the pay checks or grade cards that are always available to directors in showbusiness or the educational theatre. Our players are practicing an avocation which, while achieving important theatrical results, has also to be a pleasurable experience for them. If community theatre workers do not enjoy their work they are not apt to return.

Faced with the necessity of maintaining this happy climate, the director is also required to take an acting company of varied degrees of background and social experience and teach them in a few brief weeks many intricate points of technique. Unlike a repertory company that builds on past learning together, the community theatre cast seems at times to present an almost insurmountable teaching problem. Accurate casting leads to a large playing group, which in turn tends to bring in newcomers and beginners. In Shreveport our six annual productions use from eighty to one hundred different individuals as actors.

The good teacher is not afraid to take those with little or no experience, whereas the director who does not teach well begins to depend more and more on his veterans and, unless he is careful, the playing company narrows until miscastings appear and the evils of the stock company start to emerge. I have found it possible to concentrate a large amount of teaching into ten-minute briefings before rehearsal, and ten to fifteen minute critiques after the evening is over. I take up a regular sequence of subjects, including all the fundamentals, and present them in capsule lecture form. I also set a series of rehearsal objectives, paying particular attention during rehearsal to the topic discussed before it. In this way such matters as concentration, listening, repose, picking up cues, timing, the center of attention, continuity, characterization, and so forth, receive explanation and graphic illustration. To underline the continuous quality of our work, I often announce the subject of the next rehearsal's objective at the conclusion of the night's critique.

I make certain that deadlines for line-learning and for the end-of-prompting are clearly understood and the dates well kept. One week before we open, all prompting is stopped and we are then able to set as our objectives the final creative ones which lead the play to readiness for its audience. During this last week, the assistant stage manager makes note of any line trouble so that the players do not have to remember errors but can concentrate on keeping alive the emotional values of the scenes. After rehearsal they can check with the assistant stage manager for mistakes.

During this period we stress the basic reason for theatre, the mutual emotional experience of players and audience, and the obligation of the actors to keep that emotional line alive and continuous. They are taught to believe firmly that nothing must disturb it and that nothing so deadly as a prompter's voice can be allowed near their creative work. In more than a quarter century we have never heard a prompter's voice during one of our performances, and our actors are concerned when they find programs from other playhouses on the Green Room table carrying such titles as "book-holder" or "prompter."

Assuming that the young director is becoming qualified in his art and that he uses the most modern developments in its practice, it is now important to make certain that he develops properly outside rehearsal hours. The community theatre director's personal public relations are intricate and demanding. He faces first the skepticism with which the average man tends to regard any artist and second, the excessive public attention which follows every action of a professional theatre person.

To counteract the first he has to prove that his interest in the community and its problems is as real and sincere as the average man's. There is no choice about this, since community theatre to succeed has to become firmly interwoven with the warp and woof of civic life. Once the citizens begin to believe that the director wants his theatre to do well because it will be good for the town, the public relations victory has begun.

To live in the strong light of public attention requires a personal life above reproach. It is a tragic fact that many promising community theatre careers have failed at this point. The director cannot enjoy the freedom of conduct which may occasionally be the choice of the ordinary citizen.

He has to be careful not to limit his friendships among the people of the playhouse or he will soon be accused of favoritism. He has to please the people who may take a drink and those who would not consider it. In short, he faces the almost impossible task of leading a personal life above criticism by any of the social groups of the community.

Maintaining a good home for his wife and children fits well into the mores of a town. There have been in recent years several decisions on applicants for directorships where the talent was equal but the married man was selected because of his implied stability. With the small salaries paid by many organizations, the married man also faces an economic hurdle.

Bohemianism will not do. There are a good many towns which no longer have theatres because their director did not understand this. The average man may think it quite proper for his club to have a bar but he will not want to work in a community theatre, nor will he let his wife and children participate, if liquor comes near it. Not only does a director have to strive for immaculate personal conduct but he is required to police the actions of all his people while they are at the playhouse.

While the director is a professional man of the theatre, he has to know that his town will not care for much of the showbusiness manner. This may explain why those who try community theatre direction after disappointments on Broadway seldom last long. One such man nearly wrecked several important playhouses before he finally realized that he did not believe in the unpaid actor. He has been much happier the last few years playing bit parts in Hollywood.

Winning this double acceptability—as a capable artist and as a sincere citizen of the town—is a formidable task. That so many have succeeded is surprising and gratifying. It implies the motivating virtue of *dedication*.

Without dedication the best trained and most capable of directors may not succeed. The constant battle on two fronts, play-production and integration with the community, may seem too hard. Being both a public figure and an earnest private citizen is giving great value for perhaps a small salary. Only the dedicated can meet the challenge happily and with persistence.

With this quality present, however, community theatre directing begins to reveal many satisfying attributes. Now ahead lies a career of producing theatre in a quantity, and of a duration, impossible in showbusiness. If a director finds fulfillment in directing plays, then community theatre offers rich realization. In his own theatre and in his own style, he can have the privilege of five, six, or seven productions each season. His Broadway colleague will be lucky to average two a year.

As he grows as an artist, so will his organization grow with him. Under a good teacher his players will progress as they are able to practice their art far more frequently than the members of Actors Equity. Since actors learn to act by acting and directors develop by directing, community theatre offers the fullest and longest of training courses.

With this fulgent realization of the artistic life, there is the warm accompaniment of a normal home life. As roots deepen in the town, these values increase. One-night stands, road tours, even commuting between Hollywood and Broadway, seem nerve-wracking prices to pay for a chance to work in theatre. The average American's life is the best any citizen of any nation has ever known, and for an artist to share its sound, normal privileges is a splendid and stabilizing experience.

As a few years go by, the young directors begin to understand these double values. When the long-range attitude develops toward their organization, they and their theatres begin to grow into the civic structure. With the deepening roots, the foliage grows higher and more important overhead.

In the early years our friends in New York and Hollywood often asked, "Why do you stay out in the country?" Now, after twenty-six years, they say, "You were right." Most of them have had brilliant careers and have made lots of money, but they have missed the values we have found in community theatre.

In addition to our home and the great privilege of raising our children, Jock and Jill, Margaret and I have had the special pleasure of doing theatre *together*. As we near the two-hundred mark in our production series, we often ask, "What other couple has theatre so richly rewarded?"

CHAPTER NINE

How Fearless Can We Be?

Several busy, progressive years have now passed for our not-so-new theatre and our not-quite-so-young director. Having followed the correct procedures they have found that wide participation, the common objective of the play, and the other principles *do* work. Yet difficulties have arisen. Counting on the growing ability of their audience, they have found with some surprise that three of the season's productions did not please. They were well cast and well directed and yet the results were so disturbing that the new membership campaign is suffering.

The director, still recalling the pleasure of his study of the classics, had been particularly disappointed when Ibsen's *Ghosts* proved highly unpopular. In fact, he had heard that some of the audience had walked out at the end of the second act. This seemed strange, since the director knew how well *Ghosts* was received when his university theatre did it his Senior year. The second failure had been the first production of a new manuscript. The board felt keenly about this, for they knew how the director had tried to find the best unproduced work for their first venture with an original play. Those efforts had not been confined to the state or region; no, indeed.

The director had met several of the leading agents in New York and he had gone directly to them and they had, they said, sent him the best of their unoptioned material. The play reading committee had worked hard on the project and their decision and the director's were in agreement. The local press had been enthusiastic about the original play idea and made quite a to-do when the young playwright came for three weeks of rehearsal and rewriting. The entire project was difficult and wearing, and the board and director were understandably disturbed when they were told that a member of the audience had said, after seeing the performance, "What a waste of time! Why should our playhouse bother with a new script when they could have given us *The Solid Gold Cadillac* or *Witness for the Prosecution?*"

A week after the run was over, the director had said to his wife, "I still don't understand it. Of course it wasn't a perfect play, but you know how exciting that Workshop Series of new scripts was at the university. You'd think our audiences could take *one*." "Yes," said his wife, "but that audience at school was all faculty and students—and the performances were free."

Most upsetting of the three play problems, in a way, had been the reaction to *The Children's Hour*. There had been some discussion at board meeting about possible objections, so it was decided to take no chances. There was to be a production of the play in a city two hundred miles away, so several of the board and the director and his wife went to see it. It was done by a small, rather sophisticated theatre group, and reactions and comments about the performance were excellent. Fully reassured, the party started the drive home certain of the success they would have with *The Children's Hour*. One of the board made an interesting comment, "You know the city is exactly four times as large as our town: 320,000 against our 80,000. You don't suppose that will make any difference?"

Something made a difference, for when their production of *The Children's Hour* opened, a furore had ensued. There was much talk about the playhouse's obligation to the good taste of the community and two or three church groups had become exercised. The director heard that one citizen had not allowed his teenage daughter to see the play.

These difficulties with play selection seemed difficult enough, but the building fund drive had also run into trouble. It was the consensus of the board and the director that, after five years of successful operation, it was time to raise $75,000 for a new plant. They were encouraged in their decision by the success of two organizations in cities about the size of their own. In City A, a community theatre in its twelfth season had raised more than $60,000, and in City B, with an organization in its sixteenth year of operation, nearly $80,000 had been secured for a new playhouse. Such had not been the case with the local drive. After six months of hard work, less than $20,000 had been pledged, and workers reported that there was no chance of getting more at this time.

At this point a wise board member suggested that three months be spent in getting a correct evaluation of their organization's relation to the city and how that relationship resembled and differed from those existing in communities of similar size. This proved to be one of the most valuable projects undertaken by the five-year-old theatre and brought a number of interesting conclusions. First, they learned that while certain factors seem common to American towns of similar size, there are individual differences which often affect the course of a community theatre. The amount and type of industrial involvement, the presence of a college or university, the predominance of a racial group, the amount and length of support given to the other lively arts—these are among the traits which give a town or city its individuality.

We are rapidly becoming a nation of uniformity. Our transient population, the years of mechanical entertainment media, our dependence on nationally distributed products—all these are tending to make American towns and cities alike. Our regional speech differences are rapidly disappearing. We talk alike, we dress alike and we use the same automobiles, television sets, furniture, air conditioners; and a house in Atlanta will have many twins in Tennessee and others in Oregon. Yet there are still differences, and a community theatre should be aware of them. A town which has in its borders a great university may give its community theatre an audience with some fondness for an occasional classic. A neighboring town which has 90 per cent of its working population employed in factories may care little for the classics when it goes to the play; nor even for Shaw or Coward.

An alert board has to be aware of any personal differences in their town's nature and, if the director is not a native, keep him informed of those differences. In *The Children's Hour* incident, a serious error was made by the board and the director in assessing the success of the production by the sophisticated city group, because they failed to take into account: First that the play was not done by a true community theatre, in that it reached only a small segment of the playgoing public of the larger city; and second, that the play was not done for a family audience, nor were they interested in such an audience, as the list of their season's productions indicated.

In retrospect the mistake was obvious, since this organization was aimed at the average man and his family and Miss Hellman's splendid play was not intended for the family audience.

Obviously the matter of play selection needed more thought, but what about the failure of the building campaign? Here the second look was again revealing. The most striking difference between their organization and those in Cities A and

B was in age. Next was their difference in financial goals. Their five-year career was too short to justify an ambition of $75,000.

They looked further and saw that young community theatres in towns their size generally went through a remodeling period in their housing. Remodeling? With their pledges of $18,000 they might manage, so they lowered their sights and began to look for a suitable existing building.

Their research brought other important lessons. They saw that it is better for a community theatre to grow slowly than to risk over-expansion. The successful building programs are generally done by the organizations with a good many years behind them, years which have achieved the vital goals of integration with the town, establishing a place in the civic pattern, making the theatre *matter* to *many* people spread through the range of the town's social structure.

They discovered a few monuments to reckless financial involvement by a community theatre. In Dallas they saw the former home of the once-great Dallas Little Theatre, victim of a mortgage too large to be resolved. For some years the plant has had no higher artistic mission than showing Spanish motion pictures. A few miles away, at Tyler, Texas, they observed a handsome little building which was erected by an infant community theatre. The structure was completed but could not be kept, and in interesting compensation for the many churches which have become theatres, it now serves as a house of worship.

There are others in this band of lost playhouses, and they should serve as a reminder that building a new theatre plant is an expensive and difficult process which, if mishandled, may cost an organization its life.

This serves to underline the necessity of sound businessmen in the leadership of a community theatre, their value increasing somewhat as their distance lengthens from actual involvement in play production. Thinking in terms of what is good for the organization in relationship with its value to the community will result in more progress in certain directions than a mere passion for producing plays.

Some years ago one of our board presidents in Shreveport knew that the Playhouse needed air-conditioning and central heating. Within one season, this man, almost singlehandedly, raised $18,000 for the installation of a fine dual system. He has never been in a play nor worked backstage, but he believed in the value of the Playhouse to Shreveport. When he was elected to the board of directors, he wanted to serve the organization as he had served many others; so he found a project and completed it.

If tempering courage with prudence is important in financing, it is equally essential in play selection. There is constant temptation to be reckless here, and its most vocal sources are often self-appointed advisers from the would-be avant-garde, urging that it would be "so smart" to do *The Little Hut* or *Waiting for Godot*. In earlier years they were great boosters of Saroyan.

There are two sound arguments against the selection by a community theatre of plays in this area. First, and fundamental, is the danger of offending and losing the family audience. A few community groups, like the city company who did successfully *The Children's Hour*, are not concerned with family approval or attendance. But, like them, most of these organizations lie on the fringe of true community theatre, serving small intellectual or artistic groups which are only part of a city. By the mere limitation of their audience they tend to remove themselves from many of the true community theatre's obligations. Carry this tendency toward the "arty" play and its sympathetic audience a bit further and we are back to the clanishness and faults of the dramatic club philosophy.

Stronger perhaps than the sociological argument is the matter of true theatre and its relation to the avant-garde. Painting, sculpture, writing, and music have no real limits in their development toward either the pedestrian or the esoteric. The modern French painter can paste tiddly-winks and popcorn on a canvas and someone will come along, toss his long hair back, and proclaim that he "gets" the message. A "composer" can jot down a ditty entitled "My Ever Lovin' Polka-Dot Shoes" and some hillbilly will grab his guitar and sing it.

These phenomena occur often in the other lively arts and we cannot deny that someone, somewhere, "gets the message" because the aesthetic experience, is an individual one. The Creator has made Man in infinite variety and there may always be one who sees three marble balls as a piece of sculpture, even though the rest of us think it looks like a pawnbroker's sign. Nor can we prove that a book written in meaningless jargon does not have a few understanding "readers." Such stunts do have the questionable value of attracting attention to the "artist."

Theatre, however, because of its basic form, tends to forbid such shenanigans. It is, and will remain, a group experience, players and audience living a common emotional span of creativity. Theatre does not exist when one man sits alone in the auditorium watching a play.

If the group experience is to come alive, there has to be communication between what happens on the stage and those in the audience. The simple barrier of language is enough to prevent such communion. An audience of Americans, knowing not one word of German, will not find a true theatre experience watching a German troupe perform in their native language. The aesthetic experience of opera is in *music* so that language is no barrier. It is interesting that we tend to find operas sung in English translations less satisfactory than in the original tongue; and others have noted that some of their most satisfactory operas have been heard sitting before their radios in the peace and comfort of their homes.

Far stronger than the language barrier is the one which rises when there is no contact of *ideas*. Here is where the would-be avant-garde playwright gives himself away. When he writes a work so obtuse that only one or two profess to understand it, he has written himself out of theatre; failing to create a group experience, he has failed to write a play. What he has written should perhaps be put in cloth binding and set on the shelf next to *Finnegan's Wake*; it does not belong on a stage.

Some years ago the National Theatre Conference asked William Saroyan to write a play for which their members could have first production rights. After a time, a manuscript arrived in the Cleveland office bearing the title *Jim Dandy*. It was duly mimeographed and sent to the eighty members of NTC. As I began to read my copy, I was startled to find that the setting was "the interior of an egg." Finishing the piece, I knew that for my audience there could be no communication of idea and hence no play. However, some fifteen of my colleagues did produce *Jim Dandy* and reported that their audiences seemed puzzled.

Their bewilderment was partially explained by the cream of the jest. Some four years went by and a letter came to the chairman of NTC's New Plays Committee from Mr. Saroyan. In it he said, "I want you to know that I am now writing the play based on the *outline* I sent you some time ago." The last I heard, the finished *Jim Dandy* was as puzzling as the outline.

The most devastating blow to the self-appointed avant-garde of drama comes when they realize that their unintelligible plays will probably never find an audience. In the other arts recognition after death has come along with romantic regularity. The *Christopher Bean* plot has many real-life counterparts, where the poor painters starved and died and their masterpieces had to wait until time developed those who could understand and appreciate them. The unrecognized sculptor, composer, and writer can go to his reward with the satisfaction of thinking that some day, somewhere, there will be those who appreciate his genius. Not so with the playwright. We do not excavate musty manuscripts which could find no audience in their day and, putting them on the stage, discover that the past was wrong. Our heritage in drama consists of plays which lived in their time, although we tend through the centuries to substitute the scholar's reverence for the contemporary adulation the playwright enjoyed for being a vital man of theatre.

I like to think of the body of proven plays as being elliptical in shape. Around the center is the great bulk of easily understandable work. The passing years take away those which do not possess continuing communication. To the left the ellipse narrows as we get to the plays which are cheap, ordinary, and with little claim to artistic merit. On the right the boundaries close about the manuscripts which have restricted appeal and narrowing communication. They need the special audiences. Outside the right boundary of the elliptical treasure house lie the would-be avant-garde writings.

We are not being fearless in community theatre to work too far to the left or to the right, except as we are certain that our audiences are with us. Whenever we endanger the central purpose of our effort, the continuance of theatre, by choosing plays beyond communication with our audience, then fearlessness changes rapidly to foolishness.

Play selection for the community theatre is a constant and redoubtable problem. Here the entire effort of the organization narrows to a focal point where, if errors are too many, the existence of the playhouse may be threatened. To add to the hazards of the task, correct evaluation of a play is one of the most difficult assignments in all of theatre. The best of the Broadway producers, and the most skilled of the agents, have been unable to lower that almost constant average of failure in the Times Square playhouses, which year after year reads around 70 per cent. This happens despite access to almost unlimited money and the world's finest theatre talents. Primarily the difficulty begins with the basic form of theatre: it does not exist until the curtain rises and the audience begins to live the experience. Thus far, no genius has come along who can visualize accurately the result on opening night by reading the playwright's typewritten pages.

Another element which makes Broadway producing such a hair-losing gamble is the New York audience's hit-or-nothing attitude. This is partly due to Madison Avenue's men in gray flannel suits who advertise that we must buy only the newest and the best. This may be sound practice in purchasing toothpaste or soap flakes, but it is not only unfair to theatre, it is also illogical.

High-pressure selling techniques have made the Broadway public clamor to see the hits, and when the pressure makes tickets unavailable they refuse to attend plays which may be slightly less perfect, although still of value. Thus the Times Square audience approaches the playhouse with the object of bagging another hit for its collection, rather than to purchase tickets for the privilege of playgoing.

Unless playgoing is an aesthetic experience, it is sensible to settle for television or radio and save the money. But while group katharsis is the basis of theatre, the range of the experience within each individual depends upon the length, breadth, and depth of the life which has made him what he is. It would be impossible to assemble even five hundred persons as an audience whose life patterns matched exactly; so a play means many things to many people.

With the wide range of human capabilities in any audience, we cannot say that the hit play was necessarily a "hit" experience for all. Some of that audience might have found a more satisfactory evening, one closer to their emotional range, in the show down the street with the half-empty house. The latter had not been sold in the ads and the columns as "the newest and the best," so they did not buy it.

We have but to look across the Atlantic to see a nation which thinks more highly of going to the play than of merely annexing hits. In England people like to practice the art of playgoing and their appetites are widely developed. They support the less-than-perfect productions, the plays of merit which do not happen to be hits, and the result is that the West End is able to have twice the houses and annual productions that we can afford on Broadway.

As we become more mature as a nation we too may broaden our appetites. We may become less obsessed with looking for that which is *new* and seek that which brings *satisfaction*. We follow that path in the other arts and would think it ridiculous to see marquee lights which said, "Come in and hear the newest symphony" or "This gallery now showing only the newest pictures!"

Not all this infection of attitude came from the hucksters of New York; Hollywood is also suspect. For many wealthy years, the masterminds of the film industry reasoned that "if we can make the public rush to see the newest pictures, then we'll make more and more new pictures." The centrifugal expansion worked profitably for a time; build more houses to show more new pictures, and make more new pictures to fill those houses.

When sight began to join sound in the living-room, however, this policy of riches-through-quantity turned like a
monster upon its creator. Hollywood began to see that the
public would rather stay home and look at the old pictures
free on television than pay money twice a week for attractions
at the neighborhood movie which had only the virtue of new-
ness. The change to fewer and *better* motion pictures has
been necessary, for the public that now edges its way past the
popcorn machines is looking for quality first. This change
in the buyer has gone so far that it is possible to re-issue the
best of the old pictures at a profit.

This attitude may seep into playgoers and serve as an anti-
toxin to cool the fever for the new. Television may also unwittingly help to mature our attitude toward the play. Its
hungry maw now consumes more than four thousand program
items each week. It has already consumed nearly all the best
plays, novels, and stories. Forced to do some repeating, the
networks may find that the viewers would rather watch a
good program twice than leave the dial set on something
which is not *good,* only *new.*

These factors all bear on the problem of selecting plays for
community theatre. Looking up from his fantastic budget
figures, the Broadway producer might say, "You have no
problem. We took the gambles; we proved the plays so the
community theatres have only the process of choice."

What that producer does not know is that what is right for
Broadway may be entirely wrong for the civic playhouse.
Many of New York's greatest successes are ruled out of consideration because of subject matter or treatment. His problem
again differs in that the Times Square theatre works on a one-
play basis; the relationship of a single production to the rest
of the season is unimportant.

Community theatre programming begins with a season as a

yardstick. Balance and variety are needed through five to eight plays. The manpower for the task of selecting these plays is found in a play reading committee. Ideally it is appointed by the president from board members and should number five. Here, as with the board itself, it is well not to have members too close to actual play production. The actor on such a committee cannot be blamed for favoring plays which appeal to him as an actor, or which have only the merit of good acting roles.

Again, experience is important to this work. The starting theatre may have no one with background but, once service begins, it may be wise to continue any member on the committee through his entire board tenure; the passing years add to the value of the play readers. It is also desirable to have as wide a range of viewpoints as possible. Working always closely with the director the play reading committee should be a miniature sounding board of the playhouse audience. Particularly valuable, if they can be found, are one or two who react like the average man and his family. They will keep selections from getting too far afield in the ellipse.

The work is a year-round process with readings running from six months to a year ahead of production. Our committee in Shreveport holds about twenty-five meetings a year for exchange of books, discussion, and evaluation. We keep a chart on every play read, with recorded reactions from the five readers. A minus sign indicates disapproval for our use. A plus sign shows that it seems a possibility, while a zero mark indicates a negative reaction. As these marks accumulate, the chart begins to show the plays which seem desirable, those which could be used if necessary, and those rejected.

The professional director is the one who submits the plays to the committee. As an expert, he will tend to steer the reading to plays of some merit, and away from plays he dislikes, an obvious right of any director, professional or not.

Most organizations will find it difficult to please with the classics. Certainly classics deserve all possible production, but in most larger towns the college programs seem to take care of this need and are able to provide a suitable audience. At Shreveport we roughly define classics as great plays written before the twentieth century. We find some comfort in not producing more of these when we realize that some of the modern works we have done will be classics in the twenty-first century. Shakespeare, Ibsen, Chekhov, the Greeks, and the other masters are hard to sell in the average community situation but when they can be sold, or afforded, I am always proud and happy.

There are those who say that community theatre does not give new playwrights a chance. We have tried it and found that our audiences would rather see a play which is new to them by a *proven* writer than to see an *unproven* work by an *unproven* playwright. Community theatres do not mistrust the *new play;* we would be happy to do the first productions of any play of merit by Paul Osborn, either of the Andersons, George Kaufman and his current collaborator, Mary Chase, Howard Lindsay and Russel Crouse, Samuel Taylor, the Kanins, Rice, John Patrick, John Van Druten, and the other top dramatists.

The new work of these ladies and gentlemen is, however, safely locked behind options, or at the bottom of the pile on the agent's desk. One day that may change. If our playwrights would count the volume of community theatre productions and the resultant royalty, they might begin to think of their new work as having a long and profitable career without going through the holocaust of a Broadway showing.

So it is not the new *play* which we shy from doing, but rather the *exercises* of the new, or would-be, playwright.

Not more than twenty-five men and women make a full-time living by writing solely for theatre. Is it not rash to assume that any young person who writes something in three acts or ten scenes will really develop into a *playwright*? Should not his developing writings be more honestly projected on a stage in a university's workshop program before a free audience? Can we honestly charge full price in the community theatre for the unproven writings of an unproven writer?

A rather shadowy figure in the theatre scene, one almost resisting definition, is the local playwright. This is not the writer who has had a play produced or published, but includes all those who work, probably sporadically, at the writing of plays. With the formidable arguments against the writings of the unproved "playwright" are we to ignore his efforts and renounce all responsibility? Such a course may hold logic, but it is devoid of faith and humanity. Furthermore if we look at the record, we know that there have been enough exceptions to the rule that all good modern plays are first produced on Broadway to lend some excitement to this matter of perusing locally written plays.

No doubt William Inge would occupy the same eminence today had it not been for the Galveston incident, but I like to think that the Galveston Little Theatre's production of Inge's *Front Porch* speeded the day when the work grew to be *Picnic*.

So it seems rational to regard this added chore of attention to the local playwright as not entirely altruistic. There may well be more diamonds in the sand pits. It will be a rare occasion when the community group can find a home-town play which will justify its place on the main program; but for playhouses with workshop schedules and second auditoriums there can well be time and place for occasional full productions. Since the chief objective is to help and forward whatever talent the local writer may have, it does not seem that these often should be sold to the public. The invited audience, paying only a written reaction for the evening, was long of value at the Yale University Theatre.

An even simpler, but valid, solution is to give a promising local play a reading-rehearsal performance. This should be carefully prepared if the playwright is to get substantial aid from the venture. However, not taking the cast through the memorization period cuts the time element sharply.

From such enterprises the community theatre might well discover and improve a small number of manuscripts yearly. If the qualified director, upon conclusion of the reading performance, feels that the rewritten work is worthy of further attention he can then send it on to any of the leading agents in New York who are consistently attentive to the glimmer of fresh talent.

Among the finest accomplishments of the late Margo Jones was her steady belief in the unproduced play. True, she had access to many of the best new scripts in New York, but from her tiny Dallas arena playhouse came a succession of plays so improved by their Southwest production that they were able to face and, in some cases triumph, in the Broadway market. Among them were *Summer and Smoke, Twilight Walk* and *Inherit the Wind*.

The quest for worthy dramatic material has always been difficult. It will probably not get any easier; but we who have actors and stages owe attention to any faint glimmering of playwriting talent which may find its way to our stage door.

The best of the tested modern plays remain as the chief items for community theatre programming. This is today's common practice. There are some who accuse the community theatres of doing "warmed over" Broadway; but the approach, the methods, and the philosophy of the commercial and the noncommercial theatres are so far apart that the same play, under the two systems, usually seems different to the spectator. And the play itself tends to get a better chance away from the fanfare of the star system.

Quality, however, is not the significant point here. Since our present audiences seem to prefer contemporary theatre, they should not be denied the privilege simply because they happen to reside in Indianapolis rather than the Bronx. So long as established playwrights insist on channeling their work through Times Square, we of community theatre are forced to do our own productions of many plays presented there. We are not warming over anything; we are simply using the largest present source of contemporary drama. And we are giving our audiences their right to see the reflection of their era as it is mirrored in contemporary drama.

The director and the committee have a large assignment when they narrow their field of choice down to the best of the plays written in English in this century. As we move deeper into the hydrogen age, some of our playwrights keep trying to find the last word, or words, to shock. Situations have kept pace with the rate at which actors have been given additional four-letter words to utter. It is a temptation for a playhouse to try some of the New York hits which have, as their chief excitement, a new "shock." I hold that in our present form of community theatre we had best choose the language and the actions which will not shock our audience right out of the auditorium. The list of appropriate plays is long enough. Many of the milder plays which were quickly brushed off on Broadway have gone on to pleasing and profitable careers on community theatre stages.

This will not please the avant-garde, the sophisticates, the pseudo-intellectuals, and yet it is the majority practice in our present community theatre. Is this policy of moderation exerting a force in national and world culture? I think so.

CHAPTER TEN

A Force in National and World Culture

The rate of growth of the community theatre in America is, a matter for amazement. In less than half a century, this shy, hesitant cousin of showbusiness has become the major producer of plays. This has happened without a formal plan, a full national organization, or any standard preparation for leadership. Even today communication in the field is inadequate and in many areas nonexistent.

In spite of these many deficiencies, the community theatre idea has spread across the forty-eight states at such a pace that we cannot count the organizations. It is not that the total is beyond measure, but that added to the lack of contact between groups is the difference in development in the groups themselves. In almost any section we see playhouses in their third and fourth decades of existence and, around them, organizations in the first, second, or third year. To add to the trials of a census, the younger groups often change form, names and addresses. I recently worked on a "representative" list of community theatres and stopped when I passed the thousand mark without having touched on more than a fraction of the groups densely spread across the land.

The lack of any national cohesion in community theatre has naturally resulted in much lost motion, and in creating anew many problems long since solved. No American business would tolerate such isolationism, and even the other lively arts long ago gained the benefits of cooperation. The tiniest art gallery has access to methods long proved by use, and the newest civic orchestra soon begins national affiliation. Attempts have been made to organize the community theatres but even the latest, the National Association of Community Theatres, has met with limited success.

Despite this waste of time and motion there may be virtues in the pattern. Because each community group has gone through the rough-and-tumble of learning survival without help from a national body, the theatres which have continued have evolved a certain rugged individualism, a dominant quality in America's success story. In a time when so much of our living, our education, and our entertainment has been regimented into national patterns, the community theatre today exists as hundreds and hundreds of local structures. In many cases they hold a fresh quality mirroring their respective towns or locales.

The total impact of these separated enterprises has significance in the sum total of our national culture.

Only recent years have found us using the word "culture" without apology. As a new, young, vigorous, and successful nation, we admitted to many qualities, but we regarded culture with suspicion. Now we are wiser and know that men can be free, successful, virile, *and* enjoy the world's culture. We have come to know that painting, sculpture, literature, and music are high pleasures, well worth the seeking. The adventure has but begun for us. Denmark has more bookstores than the United States and there are perhaps more of the world's masterpieces in the Louvre than in all our galleries. This is no matter for embarrassment. With the nation as with the individual, the true acquisition of culture takes years and growth.

It is also a matter of participation, not price. Mere *ownership of* a Rembrandt does not certify cultural ability, but the tendency to spend as much *discerning time* as possible with the masterpieces in the galleries indicates a high level of aesthetic appreciation. In an era in which we are asked to accept price-tags as measures of true value, it is hard for some to acknowledge that culture is not for sale. The high snobbery of the Metropolitan opera's old Golden Horseshoe is not still a measurable item in our national cultural scene, but for the old monopoly of the *few* some have now substituted an art-for-a-price practice among the *many*. We find this attitude in such manifestations as the book clubs, and the record fad. Participation in an art form, not *possession* of its objects, is the way homo sapiens reaches the right to be called a cultured man.

The liveliness of the arts is a matter of gradation. Painting, sculpture, the ballet, music, and writing demand special talents, and some development thereof, for satisfactory participation. In the louder forms, the novice is subject to the protests of the neighbors, and incompetence in the quiet arts leads only to rejection slips and disinterest. Some approval by society is a natural desire for those seeking fulfillment in their endeavors.

Here we may find added reason for the almost illogical success of community theatre. Here is an art form which embraces or touches all the others and yet allows happy participation by a group that may include those of no artistic talent alongside those possessed of great gifts. It further invites and uses skill in the crafts, and abilities in many of our business channels. The exciting center of this broad invitation to partake is the play. From the casting to opening night there is growing public interest and recognition, satisfying that desire for all the active workers and for the organization itself.

Quite apart from the sociological benefits is the fact that, beginning with the first play, this endeavor exerts a cultural force in the town. As the season concludes and the organization moves on through the years, it becomes apparent that here, in the community theatre, are more people participating actively in an art form than are likely to be found in all the other arts of the town combined.

Not many playhouses ever think of themselves as a cultural force in their communities. Usually they are too busy to be concerned about aesthetic factors in the social structure, and most of them hold a fine humility. Yet across the land hundreds of playhouses now stand with long careers of continuous production behind them, careers which have involved hundreds and thousands of active participants.

The impact of a theatre's cultural force on its town varies generally with its age. The impact tends to be cumulative and leads to the high regard with which the entire citizenry inclines to view a playhouse which is in its third or fourth decade. The young organizations will have to understand that prestige in theatre needs to be earned. Time and sincere effort will bring respect and esteem. An organization with twenty productions behind it cannot expect the same regard enjoyed by a playhouse which has passed the two-hundred mark.

A theatre's cultural force upon its community is also subject to the factor of population. There seems to be a point in size beyond which no one community theatre can serve completely. It is hard to pin this to exact figures. We know that in the cases of the Pasadena Playhouse and the Cleveland Play House, which have developed beyond the community theatre form, large metropolitan populations brought such demands for service that they could not be met with volunteer workers. Pasadena's population has not been significant in this matter, since the Playhouse draws its audiences from the Los Angeles metropolitan area.

Somewhere between 300,000 and 400,000 the population reaches a point beyond which a single, true community theatre cannot serve a city. Cities above the half million mark seem to have many small organizations, a logical development if we accept the modern definition of a city as "a neighborhood of neighborhoods." In the largest cities, community theatre tends to be expressed in several organizations geared to serve population groups which are units of the whole. This is the answer to those who ask, "Why doesn't Chicago have a great community theatre?" and it explains why concentrated populations like Philadelphia or San Francisco will have twenty or more community theatre groups. This effect of population keeps faith with Percy MacKaye's initial premise: "There is participation, there is creative expression, there is *neighborly* ritual."

This neighbor-to-neighborhood principle has strong bearing on the next step organizationally and the larger elements of community theatre as a cultural force. Thus far, though there has been little success in efforts to organize *nationally,* and no more in attempts to set up communication lines at that level, definite progress has been made toward both objectives within *state* and *regional* areas. With speed steadily shrinking the earth, who can deny that it is easier to think of "neighborhoods" of such size?

State theatre organizations are easy to come by and many have done important work. The Louisiana association may well serve as illustrating the general pattern. In 1939 invitations were issued to the community theatres of the state to send delegates to an organizational meeting at Louisiana State University. Serving as joint hosts, the extension division and the drama department were of great help in getting the work under way. The meeting assumed the rather formidable title of The Louisiana Non-Professional Theatre Conference, and I found myself elected as the first president.

Our objectives were simple and important: to further the cause of good theatre in Louisiana by cooperation and mutual assistance. Thanks to the efficiency of Evelyn Kent Hale of LSU's extension division, our conference of thirteen member-groups was soon enjoying an imposing list of services. At the central office in Baton Rouge we maintained a play-loan library of several hundred volumes. A credit-loan system was also evolved which was of help to the smaller theatres. Upon completion of a production, any member group could send to Baton Rouge items which they would not be likely to use again, such as special costumes or properties. These would be credited to their account and would allow them to borrow items up to that value which some other organization might have deposited in the loan service. When credits did not exist, or were exhausted, reasonable fees were charged. This income allowed the purchase of lighting units which were from then on almost constantly in use.

There were state meetings annually and board meetings at more frequent intervals. A monthly newsletter was our interim line of communication. As in some other state groups, the stability and enthusiasm of the university's extension department proved the ideal motivating force, and the returns in terms of adult education alone gave them full value. The Louisiana Conference functioned until World War II, and was not resumed because of the splendid success of the Southwest Theatre Conference which was founded in 1948.

Of similar form is the Wisconsin Idea Theatre Conference which has a decade of excellent work behind it and stands as testimony to the ability of Robert E. Gard, director, to turn his dreams into reality. Working from the extension division of the University of Wisconsin at Madison, Professor Gard and his staff have proved what can be done at the state level in what he terms the "great backstage." Perhaps no other state enjoys such complete coverage of dramatic activity. Wisconsin towns with no more than a thousand population have impressive community theatre activity reaching out to include the rural areas in their "neighborhoods." The Conference elects officers for one-year terms from boards of directors who serve three years. Their publications include a quarterly, *Wisconsin Stage,* and *Shifting Scenes,* a newsletter.

Of different pattern is the New Jersey Theatre League which boasts more than seventy member organizations. They work without university assistance but have annual conferences and publish monthly *The New Jersey Theatre League Bulletin.*

One of the most successful of these projects is the New York State Community Theatre Association, which functions with the help of the extension service of the New York State College of Agriculture at Cornell University. They feature services, a publication, and an annual conference which is held at Cazenovia. A list of their sixty member groups illustrates the "rugged individualism" which has made organization slow and difficult but has given over-all strength to the idea and its propagation. A random selection of names includes: the Albany Civic Theatre, the Baldwinsville Theatre Guild, the Batavia Players, the Binghamton Civic Players, Theatre Brooklyn, St. Ann's Dramatic Society, the Studio Theatre, the Corning Workshop Players, the Fort Edward Little Theatre, the Highlands Drama Workshop, the Geneseo Community Players, the Huntington Township Theatre Group, the Coach House Players of Kingston, the Footlighters of the Calvary Methodist Church, the Pakatan Players, the Little Theatre Guild of Olean, the Play Troupe of Port Washington, the Sea Cliff Town Troupers, the Book and Candle Players of Syosset, and the Westchester Drama Association. Two names of rare flavor are, the Little Theatre of Stratford-on-Avon and the Shoestring Players!

The Ohio Community Theatre Association is another state-organization success story. With more than forty member groups, there is an annual convention and a newsworthy newsletter. Again the names are in wide variety but import the character and flavor of the state. They include: the Columbus Village Little Theatre, the Miami Valley Theatre Guild, the Coshocton Footlight Players, the Toledo Repertoire Little Theatre, the Elyria Playmakers, the Lebanon Drama Guild, the Columbus Players Club, the Sandusky Harlequins, the Trumbull New Theatre, the Springfield Civic Theatre, the Antioch Art Theatre and the Dayton Theatre Guild.

A list of other state organizations would illustrate the same point: here are neighbors on a statewide basis who have found that there are many gains in working together. The wider participation, the broader neighborly ritual, is resulting in finer creative expression.

The agendas of the state conventions do not often promise discussions of "our importance as a cultural force in the state." There are too many problems in the doing to allow much time for consideration of end results; and yet there is a greatly increased cultural impact through organization. Its rate seems almost mathematical; four theatre groups working as an organization tend to exert the cultural force of eight units working in isolation. We may accept this if we keep in mind two facts: First, theatre news tends to increase rapidly in reader interest with the numbers involved. When the playhouses of a state band together, the organization interests not only the people of the state but begins to furnish news to other states. Second, nothing does quite so much for a local project as outside approval. When activities of the Cambridge (Ohio) Community Theatre begin to be of interest to people in Toledo and Columbus and Dayton, the natives of Cambridge take new interest, find new respect, and perhaps bring added support to their town's project.

A few years ago community theatre was ready to enlarge its neighborhoods beyond state lines. This was good news for some of us in the National Theatre Conference who had become discouraged about building a theatre structure from the top down. While NTC was not interested in changing its small, individual-member format, its explorations had indicated that it was almost impossible to reach the community theatres effectively from a national structure. It was obvious that smaller units, logical geographical divisions, could have a part in the answer.

During the 1947 NTC convention the idea was at last succinctly summarized. In our room at the Waldorf, Margaret, John Gassner, and I were considering the future of the American theatre. We had remarked that efforts to pull the community theatres together at the national level seemed hopeless at this time. I felt that state organizations, while valuable, were not the complete answer, since forty-eight units would still present difficult national organizational problems.

This was when Margaret said, "The answer is in the regions, ten or a dozen of them. With reasonable distances and common backgrounds the people *will* get together. When the regional conferences are organized and running, then we're more than halfway to national unity."

This proved to be one of the National Theatre Conference's most enduring achievements. Sawyer Falk, then NTC president, spearheaded the idea of giving most of the remaining funds in the last of a series of Rockefeller grants to implement the formation of regional theatre conferences. The formation and growth of the geographical units has been encouraging, and they seem at this time to be an important step toward establishing cooperation and communication.

As with the state associations, the founding dates and rate of growth have been far from uniform, but in 1956 only one region remains without a theatre conference. The geographical divisions have tended to follow the outline set by the American National Theatre and Academy. The regional division was devised for the election of delegates to the first and second Theatre Assemblies.

The story of the Southwest Theatre Conference will serve as illustration of the general plan followed in the founding and functioning. In the Spring of 1948 Rupel J. Jones, head of the School of Drama at Oklahoma University, issued invitations for an organizational meeting to be held at Norman in October. Region Five, the Southwest, includes Oklahoma, Texas, New Mexico, Arkansas, and Louisiana.

Some forty theatre leaders arrived at Oklahoma University the last week-end in October, 1948, to set about the serious business of founding the Conference. We had little to guide us, since only the Northwest Region had met before—at an organizational meeting in 1947. We could find no constitution to follow; so Paul Baker, Ben Henneke, and myself set to work to frame one. We emerged with a document which we felt had the virtues of simplicity and clarity. It stated that the purpose of the Southwest Theatre Conference was: "To share the results of our several experiences, researches, and knowledge and, by such mutual interchange, to improve the theatre in the Southwest region."

In the intervening years, STC has worked to follow that purpose and it has enjoyed a growing membership and exerted increasing service. The 1949 convention was again held at Norman, and Rupel Jones was re-elected president. The following year Paul Baker was president and Baylor University the host organization. 1951 saw the convention at Texas Christian University and Walther R. Volbach serving as the top executive. In 1952 I was president, and the Shreveport Little Theatre became the first community theatre to serve as host. Virgil L. Baker followed me in the office and we met at the University of Arkansas. In 1954 we had joint hosts, Tulane University and Le Petit Théâtre du Vieux Carré, for the New Orleans convention, Monroe Lippman, president. 1955 found STC at Dallas with Ramsey Burch as president. There Loren Winship was elected to serve in 1956 and the convention was held at the University of Texas; the Tulsa Little Theatre was named as host in 1957, with Theodore Viehman as president.

Our annual sessions have featured panel sessions, demonstrations, and distinguished guest speakers. The Shreveport convention is typical of the format and, following the custom of an annual theme, it was built around "The Living Theatre at Home." The panel topics included Church and Drama, Avocational and Professional Relationships in Theatre, Theatre and the Press, The Drama Student Meets the Faculty, How Can STC Serve Members on a Year Round Basis?. The guest speakers included B. Iden Payne, John Gassner, Henry Schnitzler, and C. Robert Kase who represented ANTA.

Attendance at the conventions runs from 250 to 300, and publications are a *Bulletin* and a monthly newsletter. There are also various service projects and a playwriting contest which has a rather unusual feature in that the $250 prize goes to the playhouse first producing the winning play. We have felt that play contests without production were only half real. The playwright receives from the producing theatre the regular royalty paid for other works.

In 1948 the theatre people of the Southwest were mostly strangers to each other, many working with a feeling of isolation. Today they are old friends and true neighbors, helping and being helped. One who has not traveled across Region Five, largest of the fifteen regions, may not fully appreciate what it has meant to turn this vast area into a theatre "neighborhood."

Among the other conferences are the Southeastern, the Northwestern, the New England, the Rocky Mountain, and the Northern and Southern California organizations. In addition to the regional theatre conferences many others exist based upon educational theatre or speech field requirements.

The truth evident in state groupings that organization of theatre units tends to multiply many times the cultural forces exerted by the individual segments seems to follow through with regional development. In the Southwest, theatre as a cultural force began to reach real significance with the growth of the Conference.

Among my ambitions is the establishment of liaison between the Conferences. At present there is little communication between them. It is needed for two paramount reasons. First, it seems the next move toward welding the noncommercial theatre together in a national sense. Second, it will stop the growth in some areas of "regional provincialism." As I have said in some of my speeches to conference conventions, "It is no better for a region to be insular than for a state or a city. The insularity is different in degree, not in fact."

Community theatre is a powerful force in the growth of America's culture, but because of the lack of organization and communication above the regional level, we do not appreciate nor fully understand the total impact. *Life* Magazine has estimated that there are as many as 150,000 drama groups which may be roughly classed as community theatre projects. If they were a united force, their rate of progress would enjoy tremendous acceleration. Yet even in its present amorphous national form, this theatre of the people has won high praise. I have heard many of my wise friends like George Freedley, John Gassner, the late Barrett Clark, and others say, "The community theatre may well be the hope of the American theatre."

Though many of us are impatient for completion of the structure, news of what has happened since 1912 has reached far beyond our borders. Telling the story has only begun but it will continue. When the United States Information Agency in 1956 prepared its splendid packet, "The American Theatre," for use in selling the American way of life around the world, it gave attention to community theatre as an important cultural development possible under our system of government.

To millions of people in other lands, whose lives are subject to burdensome economic and political harassment, it will be good news that in the United States thousands and thousands of groups of average citizens have the time, the energy, and the freedom to make theatre. To them it will seem that a great distance has been traversed since André Antoine founded the first Little Theatre, the Théâtre Libre, in Paris in 1887. For them the stagelights across America may form a mighty beam in which they will see that a way of life which allows a people to create such a democratic cultural manifestation is rightly the hope of the world.

CHAPTER ELEVEN

What Have We to Look Forward To?

As the twentieth century is daily invented into fuller realization of the Atomic Age, the future of community theatre is bright not only because of the machines' increasing efficiency but because of fundamental conflicts between the machine and man. If we can continue to devise earth-destroying gadgets and never use them, the decades ahead may well find man for the first time in history with not enough work to go around. We listened to luncheon speakers using the word "automation" as if it were a fantastic new idea, at least a few light years away. Then we got up one morning and realized that automation was here and happening.

Now the atomic reactors, the electric eyes, the electronic tubes, and the mechanical brains are making man's labor less and less needed in volume. The thirty-hour week is not a TV comedian's joke but a nearing reality. It is wonderful that our young people are not *more* confused by these changing years. Grandfather had it so simple. He knew that if he worked sixteen hours a day and saved every penny, some day he would be a success and when he was seventy or seventy-five he might retire. Today a young man knows that if he works a few hours a day, perhaps making machine tools or running them, ahead lie pensions, retirement pay, and Social Security.

Today the leisure class does not mean those with villas at Newport and Palm Beach; it numbers millions and, in a sense, will soon include most Americans. This vast army with time-on-its-hands will want to fill much of it with entertainment. Community theatre as a logical part of that entertainment can also thank the machine for daily enlarging the potentials of the future.

Man is not conduced to similarity to his machines either by association or possession. Being a contrary organism, and a Divine one, he tries rather to find a counterbalance for too much mechanization. The golfers, the home-gardeners, the sportsmen, even the picnickers, give evidence that Americans are increasingly trying to find anew the world as it was created. The guided missiles and the space ships might well look again at the final curtain of Capek's *R. U. R.* for a lesson in ultimates. When the machines have done their worst and destroyed man and his world, humanity *does* rise again.

Some of the arts are not immune to this present passion to invent man into the position of the complete bystander. Sigmund Spaeth has written that there are those who forecast that in ten years music will be largely machine-made, with even less emphasis on the human element than in today's mechanical age.

He says, "Reports point to a future of robot rhythms and mechanized melodies in place of personal inspiration and the laborious training of the individual. The tape recorder has already made a tremendous difference in our musical life, and it was a bad day for the human equation when someone discovered that haphazard marks placed on such a surface would produce combinations of sounds that might be considered as effective as many contemporary compositions—perhaps more so."

Could it be that progressive jazz and Rock 'n Roll are but the initial punishments for our cleverness?

We have but to walk into the galleries to reaffirm how far

the painters and the sculptors have gone into the wild blue yonder of the aesthetic stratosphere. All of which seems to leave the theatre, the Fabulous Invalid, as the truest friend when man wants to indulge his humanity in art.

Through the years I have wondered why making theatre never became any easier. Margaret and I long ago agreed that the hardest production we have ever done is the one we are doing now. I think I am beginning to understand. The process of playmaking has been immune to mechanization. A few gadgets for scene shifting and light control have come along, but they have not reduced the labor required to write, cast, rehearse, direct, produce, and perform a play. For this we must be grateful. As the machines increase our nation's leisure, the time, the labor, and the participation become increasingly to be desired.

There is a pleasant correlation between the work required to make theatre and the phrase so often used to describe it: Man's most human art. The elements which make theatre are humanity in its fundamentals; human emotions, reactions, and experiences. They are what man is when you take away his gadgets and his machines. Our ability to laugh, cry, hate, love, envy, forgive, respect, despise, believe, or dissent has not changed since Euripides watched the first performance of his *Electra* in 413 B.C. If humanity endures long enough to put in commuter space-ship service to the planets, emotions and their importance to man will still have changed little.

So it is not theatre, nor its powers of endurance, which need concern us in looking ahead, but rather how we can speed the growth and quality of theatre in the United States, and particularly community theatre. From our experience since 1912, it is obvious that the greatest need has been for more capable, better-trained leadership. The educational theatres have not yet really touched the problem. The continued expansion of the school system, and the ever-present teacher shortage, are not conducive to drastic curriculum changes to prepare leaders for community theatre. It is not neatly organized like, say, the field of electrical engineering, which exerts almost a lobbying pressure on universities to produce more graduates in its area.

One day perhaps we will start further down on the educational ladder for positive action on training for theatre. It was but natural that a young nation should make its first experiment in teaching an art in the area of music. Poetry, sculpture, painting, and even ballet seemed to require a modicum of talent; but any little boy or girl could be forced to practice the piano. When the years of lessons left at least appreciation, then they had merit. The drawback was that by such long national concentration on the teaching of music we assumed that American children had no talent for the other arts.

Childrens' theatre, especially as led by the Childrens Theatre Conference, is doing an excellent job with the manpower and facilities at their disposal, but until theatre and the other arts are given academic standing, time, and equipment equal to music, we are not giving our children fully intelligent aesthetic training. Such a forward step would, perforce, have reverberations all the way up the academic organization to college trustees and state legislatures. Even they might begin to see that the surest way to prepare our future nation for the full and worthwhile use of the leisure that it *will* have is to develop talents and appreciation for *all* the arts. As the form with the widest opportunities for participation through community groups, theatre might well, one day, have the largest academic program.

Most pressing of the training problems is rapid improvement of our present methods of training directors for community drama. With the vast majority of the estimated 150,000 groups unable to think of paying a professional director, a few simple steps can still be taken to better the volunteer situations. We will have to stop thinking that anyone with any theatre talent can, by wishing, be a director. There are some groups where more time and worry is spent in deciding who shall play the leading role than in examining the qualifications of the person who will direct the play. You may have seen the inevitable results!

One of the organizations which has approached this problem with understanding and success is the Repertoire Little Theatre of Toledo. Since it was founded in 1933, it has been directed by volunteers, and yet their standards have been professional in the best sense. They use from three to five in the directing group, none of whom are paid. They require experience, either with their theatre or another. New directors are tried first in one-act programs performed only for the acting company. Fred Emmett, one of Toledo's directors, says of their plan: "Our directors' backgrounds include a complete formal education with a major in drama or allied arts. My own training included many years of stock. In twenty-three years we have done 142 productions of which I have directed 51. Mr. Hyman did 21 and Mr. Dunn considerably more than that. Ten of the directors we tried were not used again after their first play."

Here is an adult and professional treatment of the volunteer director system. Moreover this careful approach to the most important single factor in the organization has paid sound dividends. The Toledo Theatre operates on a budget running from $23,000 to $25,000 each season on the closed membership plan.

The smaller towns are not likely to have such a store of directing talent as Toledo enjoys but there are two possible sources which might serve to give the smaller organizations a set of standards and a scale of values. They would come with the spread of Samuel Selden's Licientiate degree plan as he is now building it at North Carolina University, and they would come from adoption of the apprentice-director practice by the larger community playhouses. Here again is the kind of important service project which will be functioning, I trust, when the community theatres of the United States become organized.

The way to broad affiliation is not easy and even the latest attempt, the National Association of Community Theatres, has so far failed to gather momentum. NACT, however, has one fine achievement which elucidates the great potential power which an organization of community theatres can hold. It was felt important that the 10 per cent tax on community theatres be removed at the time the new Excise Tax Bill was being prepared in 1954. The commercial theatre was naturally eager to have its 20 per cent tax removed as well. Broadway hired expert tax lawyers to lobby in Washington, while NACT had to rely on less than fifty member theatres. However, President Norman Carver asked the fifty to let Congress know their wishes; fortunately they were well scattered geographically. Of course Congress listened when their own people spoke and the new Excise Tax bill removed the 10 per cent from community theatre, while Broadway had to be content with a reduction to 10 per cent.

Our ideal community theatre includes talented representatives from all the important segments of the town or city's social structure, and civic leaders guide its policies. If this were true in but a thousand towns and cities, what a democratic and powerful national organization that thousand groups would make. It will take time to achieve this goal but one day it will happen. For the moment we may need temporary affiliation with an older national structure such as the American Educational Theatre Association. AETA would be happy to have the community theatres in a division status, much like that occupied by the Childrens Theatre Conference.

Founded in 1936, AETA has a record of excellent leadership, important projects, and many realized accomplishments. Its recent presidents include: Jack Morrison, Frank M. Whiting, Father G. V. Hartke, O. P., Horace W. Robinson, Bernard Hewitt, William P. Halstead, and Lee Mitchell. As vice-president for 1957, Edward C. Cole of Yale will become president for 1958. AETA has extended a standing invitation to NACT and all community theatres to use the division method until the day comes when the community theatre organization is developed enough to proceed alone.

The achievement of a national association would see a solution to many of the problems difficult to solve even on a regional basis. An example is the urgent need in many situations of pointing out and establishing the obligation of a city to have theatre in its civic pattern. This has been effected in many places, but it has come about only through the valiant efforts of the lone warrior, the local group.

Another item on the agenda of the future of such a national organization would be to illustrate and prove the vital role which community theatre is playing, and will continue to play, in adult education. In several state organizations, principally those backed by the extension division of a great university like Wisconsin, this fact stands strong and important. Theatre with its wide inclusion of the arts and crafts, and with its broad appeal, has tremendous potentials for furthering the education, in the finest sense, of broad segments of our population. There is a greater double gain possible than in any other area. The community theatre improves not only the individual but also his community. The personal gains in speech, poise, improvements in talents or skills, self-confidence, and art appreciation, all make the learner a better citizen. The town or city, gaining first a living theatre, becomes a finer community as hundreds of its citizens so broadly improve themselves.

No look into the future can be complete without considering the question, "Will decentralization of the commercial theatre lessen the need for community theatre?" Logically, we must evaluate the instrument which seems most likely to effect such decentralization, The American National Theatre and Academy, which has as one of its most ambitious projects The Forty Theatre Circuit Plan.

On January 3, 1935, ANTA received a Congressional Charter, the only such document ever given to an organization devoted to the performing arts. War, and tensions of war, kept ANTA from moving far during the first decade of its chartered existence, but in 1946 it announced five hundred members in thirty states. By 1957 it had about two thousand members in forty-eight states, Hawaii, and the Canal Zone. The distinguished list of ANTA's presidents through the years includes: A. Conger Goodyear, Robert E. Sherwood, Guthrie McClintic, Vinton Freedley, Helen Hayes, and Clarence Derwent. The projects since 1946 have been many, including The Experimental Theatre and the Invitational Series, the ANTA Play Series, ANTA Sponsored Productions, the ANTA Albums, The National Theatre Service, Community and Industrial Showmanship, and the International Exchange Program.

These enterprises have contained much of value, and ANTA's efforts in building good will for the United States through the International Exchange Program have been of importance. All these activities have grown from the Broadway and commercial theatre we have known for years.

ANTA's Forty Theatre Circuit Plan is the first large-scale attempt to alter that basic form and therefore presents problems of magnitude. The plan, chiefly conceived by Willard Swire, ANTA's executive director, calls for four production centers, perhaps New York, Chicago, Los Angeles, and Dallas, wherein ten plays will be produced simultaneously. These forty companies will open in forty cities at the same time, play a week, and then follow each other around the circuit.

The prime objectives are to bring the commercial theatre back in forty locations and to reduce the ninety-plus unemployment percentage among Equity actors. An operation of such magnitude will require some $5 million to get started and these funds, it is hoped, will be forthcoming from foundations and industry. When and if this great production plan will materialize is not our immediate concern, but rather what its realization will do to the existing community theatre picture. There are those who fear for survival once the Equity theatre opens down the street for forty weeks a year.

My own experience has been that motion picture versions of a play we were producing served only to increase interest in the live production. This has also been true of occasional road company showings of a play we might do the same season at the Shreveport Little Theatre. In the spring of 1955 our production of *The Caine Mutiny Court Martial* and the road company performance occurred during the same month and the proximity increased interest in both companies.

I realize that these rivals exerted far less pressure than would forty consecutive weeks of forty plays by an Equity company, but an old conviction might apply here: It is hard to have too much good theatre. Although millions of Americans are involved in community theatre, there are millions more who should have playgoing in their way of life. The more theatre we have, the better the climate for all theatre. Baseball offers a simple analogy. Things were never better for the sport than when all the minor leagues were flourishing; it seemed that there just could not be too much baseball. When the lesser leagues began to dwindle, even the Yankees could not fill the Stadium.

However the question as to whether Wichita, one of the cities mentioned in ANTA's Forty Theatre Plan, would supply reasonable audiences for forty consecutive weeks and still support its own community groups is, at the moment, academic, and may well remain so for some time. A few other matters seem to be more serious obstacles to the plan. First is the question of plays; with our current insistence on a-hit-or-nothing, where could forty hits be found for one season, to say nothing of repeating the miracle year after year? Some of the plays would be hits and deserve perhaps two or three weeks in a town, while the production following might have a total audience which could be seated in two nights; and yet the Circuit Plan would demand adherence to the play-a-week schedule.

Difficult though the plan may be, it is the most comprehensive thinking yet put forward for a solution of the constantly worsening economic situation of Broadway and the Equity actor. If it materializes, any conflicts with community playhouses will vary according to the audience potential of a city and perhaps the strength of the community group in the civic pattern. In some cases it might give a new freedom to the local group and allow them to range a bit further toward the ends of the drama ellipse, while the Circuit theatre took care of the standard fare. As a final antidote to any fears of this possible future situation, it is worth recalling our discussions of the potency of the participation factor in community drama. The average man and his family could participate in the Circuit Plan *only* through the box-office.

Another of tomorrow's questions which may find answer sooner is: "Will playwrights begin to write for community theatre?" This is already happening to some extent, as we can see by perusal of catalogs of some of the smaller publishing houses. In fact some of these lesser dramatic works have had wide production, but too often for the reasons of simplicity of production or low royalty. We have a large educational task ahead on standards.

In many cases the spirit is willing but the knowledge is weak, as with the lady who wrote me for advice on play selection. She said, "Our first year we did a one-act play; then the next season a two-act. Last year we did a three-act. Will you please send me a list of four-act plays which we may consider for this season?"

The community theatre audience is special and deserving of the best. It is for this reason that our point will not be won with the playwrights until the finest among them begin to write some of their best work toward that audience as they now write it toward Broadway. Of course we are going to need strong communication lines so that the author may be assured of many productions within a short time and his return will be commensurate with what he might have earned had he headed his play toward Broadway. When that day arrives his income may well exceed the possible New York revenue. The Shreveport Little Theatre pays an average royalty of $250 per play. If only a thousand groups matched that, the resulting $250,000 would satisfy many playwrights. I see little difficulty in motion picture or television rights being sold after a season or two in community theatre. The rate at which the ravenous appetite of television is consuming all plays, novels, and stories—classic, modern, and projected—will be full protection for any sales the author may care to make.

We may also conjecture as to whether some community theatres in the future will tend to develop into paid resident companies. This may be possible in some of the larger cities where the demand for performances exceeds the time capacity of the volunteer. If this happens, however, unionization of the house will no doubt follow and participation by the community will be right back where it was in 1910: at the box-office. In a way this might lead to decentralization of the commercial theatre, although a resident company developed in a city would not help Equity's problem.

Thomas Wood Stevens liked to think of the history of theatre as a series of waves, varying in size and height, but at each crest a golden time of acting or writing. When one is in the sea it is hard to evaluate the waves, but I sense a crest ahead. For nearly half a century we have had a new force in the American theatre. It began unobstrusively, though custodian of great ideas. Four times its purpose for existence changed, and with each change came more to participate, to learn, and to enjoy.

Today the American community theatre involves a greater total number of participants than have ever worked in an art form, in any nation, in all of history. Their numbers seem destined to increase as our American life continues toward enlarged leisure and a growing need for interesting and enjoyable avocations.

The quality of this theatre will increase only at the rate at which it can find leadership with improved training and increased dedication. Good housing will come as the average man and his friends begin to understand that few gifts make more splendid living memorials than a community playhouse bringing pleasure and edification for decades to come.

Our wave is strong. It has width and depth and height. It

is made by millions of the most talented citizens of the greatest nation the world has known.

What will be at the crest of the wave? Another era of great acting—a new Golden Age of playwrights? Or might it be simply a wondrous time for theatre, a great American theatre —expertly realized and fully understanding that "there is participation, there is creative expression, there is neighborly ritual!"

INDEX